What Really Helps

What Really Helps

Using Mindfulness and Compassionate Presence to Help, Support, and Encourage Others

KAREN KISSEL WEGELA

SHAMBHALA
Boston & London
2011

Shambhala Publications, Inc.
Horticultural Hall
300 Massachusetts Avenue
Boston, Massachusetts 02115
www.shambhala.com

This book is a revised edition of *How to Be a Help Instead of a Nuisance.*

9 8 7 6 5 4 3 2 1

Printed in the United States of America

♾ This edition is printed on acid-free paper that meets the American National Standards Institute Z39.48 Standard.
♻ This book was printed on 30% postconsumer recycled paper.
For more information please visit www.shambhala.com.

Distributed in the United States by Random House, Inc., and in Canada by Random House of Canada Ltd

Library of Congress Cataloging-in-Publication Data

Wegela, Karen Kissel.
What really helps: using mindfulness and compassionate presence to help, support, and encourage others / Karen Kissel Wegela.
p. cm.
Rev. ed. of: How to be a help instead of a nuisance: practical approaches to giving support, service, and encouragement to others. 1st ed. 1996.
Includes index.
ISBN 978-1-59030-880-6 (pbk.: alk. paper)
1. Helping behavior. 2. Empathy. 3. Compassion. 4. Meditation—Therapeutic use. 5. Interpersonal relations. I. Wegela, Karen Kissel. How to be a help instead of a nuisance. II. Title.
BF637.H4W43 2011
158′.3—dc22
2010029802

To the memory of my father
who taught me to listen

and

To my mother
who taught me to speak up

Contents

Foreword

WE MAY THINK WE KNOW how to help the people in our lives, whether they are our patients, our clients, our friends, or our family. But what is the essence of helping and supporting others? And what gets in the way of being truly helpful? Karen Kissel Wegela has written a clear, practical, and inspiring guide that answers these essential questions, drawing on her experiences as a psychotherapist, a professor of psychology, and a longtime student of Buddhism and meditation.

This book is geared toward anyone with an interest in helping, though it is especially relevant to therapists. The author introduces us to "contemplative psychotherapy" in which the focus is on how to be fully present to ourselves and others. Our presence is real and supportive when it is mindful. Mindfulness means bringing our full attention to the here and now, free of prejudice, attachment, and attempts to fix or control. This quality of presence is what is meant by openness, and it automatically fosters closeness and healing. We learn to hear and to be with others without the interferences and interruptions that come from trying to change them. We accept their reality as it is in the moment and stay with them as they experience their feelings, sit in their confusion, and wonder what to do next.

We can be present in this way because we ourselves have learned to do just that. Through mindfulness training, we become skilled at how to tolerate our own unruly emotions, uncertainty, and the challenge of going on to whatever awaits us next on our path. We have first-hand experience of the power of mindful presence, and this gives us confidence in working with others. Just staying with what is has become our most trusty tool in the face of any struggle or conundrum.

When we come to our own pain with unbiased openness, it turns into an awareness of our vulnerability, a valuable tool for intimacy. When we are open to our uncertainty we realize that it is the perfect mindset for becoming an explorer. When we face our grief, we find a tenderness in our hearts that makes us more accessible to those around us. In each instance we locate a ladder to love and happiness. We gain a new and more creative perspective on ourselves and on our concerns. We glimpse our poignant longings for love, our touching struggles, our untapped powers. This is finding the gold in our dross, an alchemical reward.

Western psychology and psychotherapy is starting to place more and more emphasis on cultivating a deep acceptance of what is and of who we are. We are not so focused on the aggressive rooting out of our flaws or the rectification of our unappealing personality traits. We are moving toward accepting the realities of our lives with an unconditional yes. We are noticing that such acceptance is actually a much more skillful means for achieving deep, lasting change. Our unconditional yes to what is, to what we feel, and to how we are with others, allows our issues and crises to yield naturally to change. The change happens as the result of loving ourselves as we are and others as they are. It turns out that loving acceptance of what is and of who we are has a *direction*. It ferries us toward transformation.

Ultimately, *What Really Helps* is a book about how to love, how to move from a narrow focus on ourselves to real contact with and care about others. In my own work as a therapist and teacher, I've come to understand that love, at its essence, is not a feeling but a way of being present. In this book we are offered practical and specific ways to be present with others, to listen and offer our help in a supportive way. Wegela also offers down-to-earth pointers about becoming more self-supportive *through* the practice of supporting others. Loving turns out to be a circle that bring us back to self-care. We notice that as we love others more truly and fully, that we love ourselves better too.

Lately, I've been working with the following aspiration in my daily life:

> May I show all the love I have
> In any way I can
> In every here and now
> To everyone on earth—including me—
> Since love is what we are—and why.

This book gives us many practical tools and insights for making this kind of love manifest in our work as therapists and in all our relationships. I hope many people will read this book and so transform our world for the better.

David Richo, PhD

Preface

THE FIRST EDITION OF THIS BOOK was published more than a decade ago, under the title *How to Be a Help Instead of a Nuisance*. I wrote it to show how Buddhist principles, particularly the teachings on mindfulness, could be useful to all kinds of helpers, including psychologists, social workers, healthcare professionals, and really anyone who would like to help and serve others. I have been delighted by the responses that I've received over the years from a wide range of readers who have found these basic teachings helpful to their particular situations.

I've heard from pastoral counselors, elementary school teachers, college faculty members, psychotherapists, lawyers, nurses, doctors, and other professional helpers. I've been especially pleased to hear from non-professional helpers: an artist with an ill father, a father of an autistic child, a beautician, a waiter, a copyeditor, a car salesman, and the parents of three rambunctious sons, among others. I have found these teachings so beneficial in my own life, and I was thrilled that they have been helpful to others as well.

I was surprised and delighted when Eden Steinberg, an editor at Shambhala Publications, suggested re-releasing this book with a new title and cover. Lately, with increasing attention being paid to the practice of mindfulness and to Buddhist approaches to psychology, the time seemed right to reissue the book and contribute to the developing conversation about the benefits of mindfulness.

This book's original title, *How to Be a Help Instead of a Nuisance,* was a bit tricky. How many people think of themselves as being a nuisance? Not many. And, even worse, who would want to receive a book as a gift that might seem to suggest that one was a nuisance!

Of course, wanting to be a genuine help to others doesn't mean that you'll become a nuisance. I hope that this book finds its way into the hands of those who will enjoy it, learn something new from it, and, in turn, be of assistance to the many beings who so deeply could use help.

Acknowledgments

THIS BOOK WOULD NEVER HAVE COME into being without the help of a great many people.

First, I would like to acknowledge the people who have allowed me into their lives as their therapist. They have generously taught me a great deal both about how to help others and also about myself. I am grateful too to the hundreds of students I have worked with over the last twenty-five or more years.

Without the urging of Louise Fabbro this book would never have been begun. Louise has insisted for the last eight years that I have been writing a book despite my repeated assertions that I was not.

Edward M. Podvoll, M.D., the founding director of the contemplative psychotherapy program at Naropa University, taught me much about how contemplative practice needs to underlie the attempt to offer compassionate help. In addition, I have had the good fortune of working with many creative and dedicated colleagues. Many of the ideas in this book come from our efforts to articulate to each other what contemplative psychotherapy is.

I wish to thank my friends and family for their affection and encouragement.

I am particularly appreciative of the colleagues, friends, family, clients, and students who have contributed their stories to this book.

Emily Hilburn Sell, my editor at Shambhala, has been a kind and clear voice throughout this process.

My gratitude goes, of course, to my husband Fred, who has been a steady, unflappable, and loving support through both the rapid outpourings of my ideas and the slow mudflows of my confusion.

I am indebted, too, to many generous teachers in the Tibetan Buddhist and Shambhala traditions, especially Dzigar Kongtrül Rinpoche, Thrangu Rinpoche, and Pema Chödrön.

Finally, and most importantly, I wish to gratefully acknowledge the compassion and wisdom of my root teacher, Chögyam Trungpa Rinpoche, the founder of Naropa University, who inspired and initiated the development of contemplative psychotherapy.

I hope that this book may be of benefit to others.

Introduction

I WAS WALKING DOWN FIFTH AVENUE in New York City one summer after I had been living for a number of years in Colorado. Although I am a native New Yorker I had forgotten how crowded the sidewalks were and how quickly everyone moved along them. Since I am not very tall, I couldn't see very far ahead. Suddenly there was a truck in front of me backing out of an alley into the street. I stopped to let it go by. It didn't seem like a choice particularly. It was a *very* large truck and I just stopped without thinking. Several people bumped into me from behind. Others streamed around me and continued on their way past the back of the truck without missing a step. One man who had collided with me—a middle-aged man in a business suit—said to me in a kind voice as he slid around me, "Never stop!"

I was thoroughly amused by his advice. Later I realized that this stranger was trying to help me. This very brief encounter stuck in my mind as an example of how readily we try to help each other. Even in the midst of a crowded Manhattan street this stranger had offered his advice on how to survive without getting crashed into.

Lately I have been paying particular attention to how often

we try to be helpful to each other. That help can range from the nearly incidental, like the example above, to long-term and profoundly compassionate help like the assistance we might offer to those in great pain or to the dying. In between lies a large range of occasions on which we might offer or receive help from others.

To be human is to interact with other people. Many times as we relate to others—both those we know well and count as friends and those we may never have seen before—the desire to be helpful arises in our hearts. In a way, nothing is more simple or basic, yet many times we don't know how to go about it. We may want to help, to extend comfort, support, intelligent help, but we don't know what to do. Many times we feel tenderness of heart when we hear about another's difficulties. We hear that a friend has been diagnosed with HIV and we want to help. We have a colleague who has just had a miscarriage. Our hearts ache when we hear of these troubles, but we don't know what to do. We don't know where to begin. We don't want to interfere or to be a burden.

Sometimes we rush in with suggestions like "I know this great doctor who organizes groups for people who are HIV positive. You should call him." Or we try to cheer the person up, saying, "Oh, you can try again. I'm sure you'll carry a baby to term next time." Or we tell the people in pain about our own experiences, assuming that theirs are the same. "When I had a miscarriage, I felt just awful for a few weeks and then I suddenly felt better. You know, I think it was mostly hormonal." To our dismay, these strategies often lead to the other person becoming quiet or angry. We wanted so much to alleviate their suffering, and yet we find we've made things worse.

My father died quite recently. A couple of weeks earlier, I had become increasingly aware of the reality of his approaching death. This prospect was a very painful one for me since Pop had always been available and supportive to me. In many ways his ability to listen to me when I was growing up, and not to impose his judgment, was the model I still carry of how to be an attentive listener as a psychotherapist. My relationship to him had long been part of how I had defined myself. Fear of what would happen when he died, helpless grief as I imagined his pain, sadness at losing him, gratitude for all he had given me—all were arising sharply and frequently.

The crisis brought many members of my far-flung family into contact. During a telephone conversation with one of my cousins, I was feeling touched and tender at this renewed connection with my family. As I told her that I was appreciating our being in touch with each other, my eyes began to tear up. When I mentioned this she said, "Don't let it get you down. Why don't you go get one of those neat cups you have and get yourself some tea?" My tenderness transformed immediately into anger. I was outraged that my softheartedness was seen as a problem and that I was being told how to fix it. In confusion, I retorted, "Don't give me advice!" I hung up feeling as if I had stomped on something precious and fragile and had lost the sense of connection I had so recently appreciated. My heart hurt. I felt worse than before. As for my cousin, she had probably heard the pain in my voice and was trying to reach out through the phone lines to offer some kind of assistance. Having her suggestion met with such a sudden sharpness may have left her feeling hurt, bewildered, and foolish.

Other times, we find that we feel so uncomfortable being around those who are experiencing pain or illness that we somehow don't get around to seeing them. We intend to visit a friend in the hospital, but mysteriously we have many errands that get in the way. It gets too late and we end up not going. Or a good friend is going through a divorce. She is often tearful and sometimes angry. We feel awkward when we are with her and avoid talking about anything that might bring up the separation. We invite her to the movies so we won't have to talk.

What is helpful? When someone is in pain, what *can* we do that is actually beneficial? How can we prepare ourselves to offer genuine help and, at the same time, to be able to be with others who are in pain?

Lately I have been asking my friends, colleagues, students, and clients the question, "What things have others done for you or said to you in your life that have been genuinely helpful?" Many of their answers have pointed to extremely simple actions. For example, one woman told me about a friend of hers accompanying her to the doctor for some tests that were frightening to her. Then the friend drove her home and made her a tuna-fish sandwich with lots of mayonnaise. They waited together to hear the test results.

Another woman told me that having a therapist say to her, "It sounds like it was pretty dangerous growing up in your home," helped her to stop feeling like she was a big baby to have felt frightened of her abusive brother. The therapist's words said to her, "You're not crazy. It was a dangerous situation and being afraid made sense."

Many tell of the importance of friends just "being there" for them. Others relate things people did or said that were surprising but that woke them up. Throughout the book I will include many of their stories.*

Helping is a very personal thing. What helps one person might not help another. What helps one time might not help again. What I can offer might not be what you can offer and vice versa.

A mindfulness-based approach to helping teaches that in order to be capable of benefiting others, we need first of all to deal with our own confusion—our own lack of confidence, our lack of clarity, and our fear of pain. To be helpful to others, we

*Throughout the book the names of some people have been changed to protect their privacy. Sometimes stories have been slightly altered for the same reason.

need to begin by working with ourselves. This principle underlies what is known as contemplative psychotherapy. This approach to practicing psychotherapy is founded on the wisdom traditions of Buddhism and Shambhala (a secular meditation program with its origins in Tibetan culture), on one hand, and the Western tradition of psychotherapy, on the other hand. While contemplative psychotherapy is specifically designed to work with those whose distress requires the assistance of professionals, many of its insights are applicable and useful to all of us.

The premise of this book is that the most valuable help we can give to another begins with developing our ability to simply *be*. What I most deeply wanted when I spoke to my cousin on the phone was to be met by her presence. I didn't want her to take away my pain or to invite me to wallow in it. I had been touched by our renewed connection and it was really the connection itself that I was craving. I just wanted her to be with me.

You may think, Be? I know how to be. I can't help but be! That's true. At the same time, most of us spend most of our time not being aware of being. We don't feel our bodies. We can stand up after watching television for a while and suddenly notice that a leg is asleep. We hadn't noticed. Or we can be so caught up in worries that we miss our exit on the turnpike. You can experiment with this right now. Put this book down and turn your attention to what you are experiencing in this very moment. Just sit as you are and notice that you are breathing. When you lose track of the breath just gently come back to it.

How long did it take before your mind wandered off? For most people it is quite soon! Usually, in our lives, we don't even notice that we have wandered away. What could be simpler than being right here in the present moment? Yet, when we start to pay attention, we find it is also one of the most rare and even difficult things to do. If we wander off so easily when nothing much is happening—like sitting here reading a book—

how much more easily do we "space out" or get lost in our thoughts when we feel uncertain or uncomfortable?

Without the ability to be present with another who is in pain, none of the techniques of psychotherapy or any other helping approaches go very far. In fact, the most challenging part of my work as a psychotherapist is not diagnosis or making insightful interpretations. Rather, it is being present along with another human being who is experiencing pain and distress.

When we really are present with someone who is in pain, we usually begin to feel pain ourselves. When I sit with a client who is sad, I may begin to feel sad myself. I may begin to feel a heaviness in my chest and my eyes may start to feel wet. When a client is angry, I may begin to feel heat rising up the back of my neck, my jaw may begin to clench. I may start to have thoughts of wanting to hurt someone.

If I am uneasy with that sadness or anger or unwilling to experience it for any reason, I will most likely mindlessly shift the conversation so that I will feel less uneasy. This shift can be very subtle. Maybe the client won't even notice. But chances are she will start to feel not much is happening in therapy and will soon stop coming. If I can't be with the client, it doesn't matter how much training I've had in how many wonderful traditions and techniques.

The same is true for all of us when we want to be helpful. The first step is becoming able to be present with someone else. As the contemplative approach suggests, we begin by learning to be with ourselves and with all of our emotions, moods, thoughts, and states of mind. The primary method for learning to do this in the contemplative approach is the sitting practice of mindfulness-awareness meditation practice, introduced in chapter 3.

The cultivation of mindfulness, attentiveness to the details of experience, is the first step. Along with developing mindfulness, we can also cultivate what is known in Tibetan Buddhism as *maitri.* Maitri (pronounced as though it were "my tree") is a warm and friendly attitude that we can bring to ourselves and others. We have a tendency in the West to judge our own experiences. We could even say that we tend to be pretty self-critical. For example, in the little exercise of noticing the breath, many people start to give themselves a hard time if their minds wander off. "I should be able to pay better attention than this! I must be some kind of moron. Now, I'm going to stay with my breath, dammit." If we forget something, if we break up with a lover, if we don't get a job we applied for, we are quick to be critical of ourselves or to blame others. An attitude of maitri means that we could simply notice what we are thinking and feeling and sensing and not judge it as good or bad. We could let our experience be what it is—we could see it clearly and not judge it further. We may or may not decide to take some kind of action, but to begin with we can see what is happening with mindfulness and with maitri.

The ongoing practice of sitting meditation also leads to the development of courage or confidence. We find that we *can* experience all our emotions; we *can* tolerate uncertainty and confusion when they arise; we *can* be bored and not go crazy. We can even experience joy and not rush to turn it into something more familiar. Developing the precision of mindfulness, the warm heart of maitri, and the unshakability of courage forms the ground for extending compassionate action to others.

The special meditation practice of *tonglen,* introduced in chapter 7, provides a training ground for gradually extending our compassion so that we can recognize and be touched by the suffering of others and still be able to remain present. Together with mindfulness-awareness meditation it provides the ground—being able to be with others, with our hearts open.

Once we can be present, then we can help in many ways. Another premise of this approach is that each of us contains what has been called brilliant sanity. The contemplative approach suggests that our most basic nature is open, clear, and compassionate. Within all states of mind are the seeds of these qualities that we can offer to each other. Not only can we offer our own resources to others, we can also help other people to tap their own richness. Learning how to do this forms the body of this book.

In the contemplative approach, helping occurs in a cycle. We begin by moving inward first, contacting our own resources and clarifying our intentions and understandings. This is followed by movement outward as we extend ourselves to others through genuine relationship and taking action. It is similar to the rhythm of the seasons. In the fall we gather the harvest and discover the resources we have to take us through the winter. In the quiet of winter we can turn our minds to inner contemplation. Then, in the spring, we begin to move outward again and reconnect with the reawakening earth. In summer we find ourselves engaged in the bustle of activity. As fall returns, the cycle begins again. In the cycle of helping, too, activity is followed by settling down again with ourselves, reconnecting and examining what has occurred.

The sections of the book follow this cycle of helping. We begin with the idea of brilliant sanity. In particular, we will look at five kinds of wisdom whose seeds are already present in us and how we can nurture their development. Part 1, "Cultivating Openness," introduces what this means and how we can explore its relevance for ourselves. Part 2, "Appreciating the Richness of Experience," is about the preparations we make to be helpful. This preparation includes making friends with ourselves, discovering our resources, and letting go of what is no longer useful.

Part 3, "Seeing Clearly," continues the inward rhythm. Having settled down with ourselves, we look deeply into our own minds and experience. One of the things we find is a compassionate longing to alleviate others' pain. In this section we explore this longing and how it can become distorted, causing us to create problems instead of to provide help. We will also look at how confusion arises. By beginning to understand how confusion takes birth, we can become more helpful to ourselves and to others when we and they become overwhelmed and upset.

After this movement inward, the cycle of helping moves outward. Part 4, "Expressing Genuine Relationship," is about what happens when we are truly open and welcoming to others. The main issues in this section are the skills of genuine communication and exchange. In the contemplative approach "exchange" refers to our direct experience of others and their pain.

Part 5, "Taking Action," continues our movement outward as we examine helpful actions and ways of working with others. It also includes how we, as helpers, may find help for ourselves when we become confused or burnt-out.

The book ends with three appendices. The first offers advice on when to bring in additional help. This is followed by a section that describes the contemplative psychotherapy training at Naropa University. Finally there is a list of places to contact for further information regarding meditation as it is presented in this book.

While many of us are "helping professionals"—doctors, nurses, psychotherapists, teachers—all of us are helpers, with or without formal credentials. Parents with children, adults with aging parents, supervisors with employees, neighbors, friends, colleagues, relatives—all of us are called upon to help when there are problems, when others seek our advice in making decisions, when others feel confused or in pain. Garage mechanics, ticket agents at airports, athletic coaches, camp counselors, bus drivers, sales people, policemen—all find themselves confronted with people who are distressed and "freaked out" when their plans go awry, when someone is hurt, when events become challenging. When relatives, friends, and even strangers are sick and dying or confused and distressed, many of us would like to truly "be there" to help both the one in pain and those close to them. It is my hope that this book will provide some useful guidance for both those who are helpers by profession and those who are helpers by avocation.

Part One

Cultivating Openness

1
The Discovery of Space and Brilliant Sanity

AS WE GAZE OUT AT THE SKY on a clear night, we can let ourselves ponder how it stretches out beyond the boundaries of our imaginations. We can never find the end of the sky, the end of space. When we try to find the root of our longing to help others, we can look deeper and deeper into ourselves, but we never can find it. Trying to find our brilliant sanity, the source of our compassionate longings, is like looking out into space. We can experience the vastness of space and the profundity of our compassion, yet we can never find their limits.

In this first section of the book we begin our exploration of our brilliant sanity. We will look at how to recognize it in ourselves and others, knowing that we can never completely capture it or reduce it to words.

Space

We can start our investigation of brilliant sanity by looking more closely at the notion of space. Usually, when we think about space in the ordinary sense of the word, we talk about how there's enough space or there isn't very much space. We think of space as something empty—a vacuum or void—into which we put substantial things. Then, we regard the things themselves as different from the space. For example, this room that I am sitting in as I write is a rectangular space into which I have put myself and my desk, my computer and printer, a lot of plants, a sofa and chair, a table, a rug, books, and so on.

Thinking of space in those terms from a psychological perspective, we might engender a sense of absence, a feeling of emptiness, or, perhaps, of boredom. We might wonder if this is what death might be like. Considering space this way might bring with it a feeling of fear, a fear of nothingness: I'll die and there'll be nothing.

Often when nothing seems to be happening, we try to fill up space, to fill up what we perceive to be emptiness. We fill our time with lots of busyness, lots of plans, lots of activities. If we run out of activities we start to feel uneasy. We tend to relate to space as a problem. As a result, we tend to struggle, so that we will not have to experience space (which we think is the same as nothingness).

However, struggling with space doesn't work, because our very nature, and the nature of all phenomena, the nature of everything, is space. Our minds are space, and so are our bodies and the environment. Everything, if you look at it closely enough, has the quality of space. What are we talking about here?

Are we talking about nothingness? Or are we talking about something else? If we look carefully at our experience we will see that we are talking about both. There are two aspects of space: emptiness and fullness.

One aspect of space is similar to this quality of nothingness, in that space accommodates other things. It's like the sky. The sky can have all kinds of things happening within it—sunshine, hurricanes, lightning, eagles, balloons, and satellites. None of those things harms the sky, harms the basic space. Space itself can accommodate anything, and, in that sense, is indestructible.

Our minds also have this quality of being able to accommodate anything. We can accommodate all kinds of thoughts and emotions: happy thoughts, depressed thoughts, angry thoughts. From the point of view of space, all experiences are equal. A thought of harming someone is no different from a thought of eating a gumdrop. From the point of view of space, with respect to this aspect of emptiness and accommodation, anything could happen in our minds. There's room in our experience, in our awareness, in the space of our minds, for any kind of experience.

Related to this sense of space as empty is silence. We could say silence is space at the level of speech. We might find that we relate to silence in much the same way we do to the emptiness aspect of space. We might tend to avoid it, or to fill it up, or to be fearful of it. With the body, space might be like stillness. We might feel uneasy being still—we might want to make something happen, to start some activity to distract us from space, silence, and stillness.

So that's one aspect of space: openness, emptiness. The second aspect of space, which differs from our conventional notion of space, is that space is also full. It is perpetually manifesting phenomena. It is perpetually pregnant. It's always giving rise to experiences of all kinds and to all phenomena as we know them: body, speech, and the activities of mind. Everything we experience arises out of that basic spaciousness, which is the quality of our mind and the quality of all that exists. Thoughts, emotions, and sensations come and go in the mind.

Our experience comes seemingly out of nothing, yet it still comes. If our minds were empty, vacant, then nothing could arise. However, there is always within us the possibility for something to arise. This understanding is very important for people who work with others, because if we think we're trying to create health or produce sanity or inject clarity it won't work.

We can recognize sanity and health because the possibility for them is already there. They are potentially there in any moment.

The Qualities of Brilliant Sanity

In contemplative psychotherapy we talk about this potential as "brilliant sanity." In the Shambhala teachings it is known as basic goodness and in Buddhism as Buddha nature. All of these are pointing to our most fundamental nature—who we most truly are.

Sometimes people ask me if brilliant sanity is the same thing as God or what some in twelve-step groups mean by a "higher power." I don't really know the answer to that. It may well be what some people mean by those terms, and it may be different for others. I think people have to decide for themselves if the notion of brilliant sanity is true for them and also if it is the same as their own beliefs about what is most fundamentally or spiritually true.

The suggestion that the teachings on brilliant sanity make is that each of us is basically, fundamentally, unconditionally brilliantly sane. What does that mean? To begin with it means that who we are is like space as I've been describing it. Our minds are like space itself: we are open and accommodating on the one hand and we are full of potential arisings on the other hand. With respect to our brilliant sanity we usually talk about three qualities. The first of these is the idea of openness as we have already discussed it. The next two have to do with the fullness side of things.

The second quality of brilliant sanity is clarity. This means that we can experience whatever arises directly and completely. For example, I have been experiencing a lot of grief since my father's death. To call it "grief" is to give a name to an experience I have, but I have to use some kind of language. The actual experience is of fullness, tightness in my chest, sadness, warmth, and tears. Along with that often come specific memories of words that we may have said, images of faces and places.

Clarity refers to my ability to simply experience all of that as it arises in the empty space of my mind and as it dissolves again. These experiences arise sharply and vividly, even painfully. Then, they shift and change—the memories run by, the words get noticed. Then it all dissolves again, and I am aware of sitting on my chair in the present moment.

Clarity refers to the quality of vividness, not to some kind of accuracy. For example, it does not mean that my less than twenty-twenty vision would suddenly become perfect if I were in touch with clarity.

I had a friend whose brother, Eddie, was a painter. He told me one day how Eddie taught him to see colors. We were driving past a field in New England during the autumn as he told me about Eddie. My friend pointed to different areas in the field. "See, over there it's kind of rust colored, and closer to us, it's more of a beige or tan? Eddie showed me how to look. I used to see it all as hay colored." As I listened I began to realize how I hadn't really been seeing the colors in the field. I had been making assumptions about what I thought was there instead of taking in what I really could see.

So clarity refers to our capacity to see, hear, taste, touch, and smell our own perceptions just as they are. It also refers to our ability to recognize thoughts, emotions, and images in our minds. We could understand clarity to be awareness itself. Not only are our minds accommodating and empty, but they are also aware, awake. This is the second quality of brilliant sanity.

The third quality of brilliant sanity is warmth. Sometimes it is called compassion or tenderheartedness. Along with our ability to be aware of our experience vividly and fully, we have as part of our nature a touchability, a softness. We are, by our very human nature, soft and compassionate. It is this quality that leads us to read a book about how to be helpful. We truly want to alleviate the suffering we see around us. It hurts us when we see a child crying, when we hear the sharp yelp of an injured animal, when we see someone being treated unkindly.

Sometimes the evidence of our compassionate nature appears as a turning away when we see another in pain. "I don't want to hear about it!" we might say when someone starts to tell us gossip about another who is experiencing tremendous suffering and hardship. We cover our eyes during the scary part of the movie. We become impatient when coworkers tell us how they really are when we ask, "How are you?" These seemingly heartless reactions come because it hurts, we are touched, when someone else is in pain. Our heartlessness comes from our vulnerable and tender hearts. Perversely, we try to shield ourselves because we are connected and compassionate.

On the other hand, we often overlook our own comfort to tend to others' needs: parents get up in the night for their children, nurses work long hours for their patients, people walk their dogs in the cold.

When my dog, Molly, was near the end of her life, I had to go away and leave her with a friend. The elaborate instructions I left for him included such things as turning her over in the middle of the night, carrying her outside to pee, arranging the furniture so she would not get stuck (she couldn't back up or lie down by herself anymore), giving her several different medications, and preparing special food. Neither he nor I gave these instructions a second thought. Molly needed this kind of help, so we gave it. And he hadn't even known her before.

Sometimes what we cannot manage to do for ourselves, we are able to do for another's benefit. For example, women in abusive relationships who will not leave their partners for their own sakes will often do so for their children's. This desire to be a benefit and not a nuisance brings many people to clean up their own acts. These days I have heard many people say something along the lines of that you can't give up bad habits, like addictions, for anyone else. You have to do it for yourself. It hasn't been my experience in working with others that this common wisdom is always true. Our natural compassion is very strong and runs very deep. If we truly want to help another, we can do a lot. If we are hoping for something back, it might backfire, but if we are in touch with our compassion, we have great strength.

My sister smoked cigarettes for years. Then, one day she gave it up and never went back. I asked why. "Debbie asked me to." Debbie is my niece. Apparently she had asked many times, but this time my sister had really seen the pain that Debbie felt about her smoking. The tears in Debbie's eyes somehow got through to her when logic and coercion had not. Joie gave up smoking to ease Debbie's pain. Debbie helped Joie to give up smoking because of Joie's compassionate heart.

So, these are the three qualities of brilliant sanity: openness, clarity, and compassion. They are unconditional. They are our nature no matter what is going on. If we are sick or well, confused or awake, psychotic or not, we are still brilliantly sane. Whether we believe it or not, whether we feel it or not, still it is our nature.

When we can bring openness, clarity, and compassion to our experience—no matter what that experience is—then we are tapping into our basic brilliant sanity. In any moment this is possible. We can always touch our brilliant sanity.

2
Being Present

"WHEN I WAS IN THE HOSPITAL, three of my friends brought me a card and some magazines. I was there for five days. Something they did that was really helpful to me was they *stayed* for about a half an hour after the nurse told me that I had multiple sclerosis. I was unable to talk." A former student related this to me.

As has already been suggested, the most important thing, when we are trying to be helpful, is to be present. It sounds so simple, yet it is one of the most difficult things to do. In the introductory chapter we took a look at how quickly our minds become distracted from being present. In the contemplative approach, the formal practice of sitting meditation is used to help us become more present to our own experience and to that of others. Formal sitting practice is introduced in the next chapter. First, here are three exercises that highlight our tendency to not be present. We can do them any time. I've included them because they are good for helping us see some of the subtle ways we interrupt ourselves from simply being where we are.

Aimless Wandering

Take a walk for about thirty minutes and let yourself notice your sense perceptions: seeing, hearing, tasting, smelling, and touching. Let yourself notice things as though you are experiencing them for the first time (which, of course, you are). Generally, it is better to do this exercise without any particular destination, just let yourself wander and see where you go. If you get lost in thoughts and lose track of your sense perceptions, gently return to noticing them.

Afterward, think back on your experience. Notice which perceptions you tuned into most of the time. Notice whether you spent more time in your thoughts or in your senses. Notice how you feel now that you have done the exercise. Some people find this a good way to relax.

Mall Practice

To do this exercise, you need to go to a place that has a lot of activity. I've suggested a shopping mall, but a bus station or any busy place would also be fine. Read the following directions before you go.

Find a spot to sit or stand where you can simply observe the changing flow of activity. Now take a posture that you can hold for a while. Being upright but relaxed usually works. Let your eyes rest in the center of their sockets and allow your breathing to be natural and uncontrived. Spend a few minutes just resting like this. When your attention wanders, gently bring it back to your posture, your eye gaze, and your breathing. Do this for about five minutes. The timing doesn't have to be exact.

Now shift your attention slightly so that what you are paying attention to is the movement of people (or anything else) as it passes in front of your eyes. Let whatever is happening in your visual field just simply occur. Don't move your eyes to follow people as they pass by. Let them come into the field of vision in front of you, and let them pass out of it again. Do this for about ten minutes.

That's it. That's the exercise. Now notice what happened for you. Did you notice any tendencies to want to follow particular colors or shapes? Were handsome men and attractive women hard to "let go"? Did you have preferences for something happening as opposed to times when no one was passing into your field of vision? Did you find yourself spacing out? Was there any pattern to this?

The point of this exercise is to start us noticing that when we are silent and still, we are still quite busy manipulating our perceptions—in this case, our sight. Each time we choose to follow that cute child as it runs across the field of vision, we are not present for what is happening in front of us. The child here is a metaphor for clinging to the present moment rather than letting it dissolve, allowing us to be present for the next moment.

Partner or Mirror Practice

This exercise was invented by some of my students at Naropa University. In my classes, students sit in two lines facing each other to do the exercise. However, you could do it with just one other person. You could even do it in front of a mirror set at the right height. It is a lot like the mall practice, but instead of keeping your head still, this time you turn it slowly from one side to the other, taking five minutes to complete a full arc. Sitting opposite your partner, you both begin by turning your heads to face the same wall. Then, you both slowly turn your heads, letting your eyes rest in the center of their sockets. When you get to the midpoint you should be facing each other (or your own reflection). Then, you continue to complete the turning of your head to the other side.

Many students find that this exercise is more challenging than mall practice. They are much more likely to get caught up in planning whether or not they will look directly at the other person, whether they will smile or not and so on. Also, they have many thoughts about what the other person might think about them. As they get more caught up in thoughts they are likely to lose track of their sense perceptions. There is often a lot of laughter afterward as people relax from feeling the tension of the exercise.

The mall exercise shows us how easily we manipulate our experience and how often we are not present. When we do the partner or mirror exercise, most of us realize that we have a more difficult time remaining present with another person than we do when we are by ourselves. Even if we use a mirror we tend to get mentally active in ways that distract us from being simply present.

The Challenge of Being Present

How can we train ourselves to be more present, especially with others? The formal practice of sitting meditation helps us become more at home with being present with our own experience. To become more at home with others becomes easier when we are more at home with ourselves. The biggest obstacle to being present with others is our discomfort with what we feel ourselves. So the more familiar we can become with all our different ways of being, the more present we can be for others.

For example, if we can tolerate not knowing what is going to happen, then we may be able to be helpful to someone dealing with uncertainty. A number of years ago I had just started going out with a man I was particularly attracted to. Like all beginnings the situation had many more questions than answers. I sat down with a friend to sort things out. Would the relationship continue? Might we marry? I easily got caught up in creating possible scenarios of how the relationship might go. Would it end soon? Would he even call again? Would I spend the next few years in this relationship only to have it end?

In this all-too-common situation, if my friend couldn't tolerate my uncertainty, she might have jumped in with inappropriate advice or gotten distracted in some way. She might have changed the subject. She might have aborted the opportunity either for me to discover for myself what was most helpful or for her to say something that might actually be useful. What was happening in the present moment was uncertainty, longing, and fear. If her responses took me away from that, they would just add more spice to the cauldron I had brewing. If she were to make suggestions about how to pin down this new man or brew up more fantasies about what might happen, she would just be helping me stir the pot. As it happened, she managed to just listen and be there. I stopped myself with a laugh, "Boy, am I getting ahead of myself."

"Yes," she said, "next thing you know, you'll be naming the grandchildren!"

Because she had experience in sitting quietly with herself, learning to be with her own uncertainty, fear, and longing, she was able to be with me with mine. (As things turned out, I did, in fact, marry Fred.)

At the same time, we also need practice in being with others so we can get more familiar with what comes up when we are with others that doesn't come up when we are by ourselves. We need to be around other people even if all we are trying to do is get to know ourselves. How much more important this becomes when we are aspiring to help others! The idea that we can live a solitary existence and then come out and be helpful to others is probably a fantasy. To be helpful, we have to learn how we are with others and what gets in our way of connecting with them. We can learn a great deal by combining an ongoing sitting meditation practice with frequent interactions with other people.

The tonglen practice introduced later in the book is also a helpful training ground that gives us the opportunity to work with all the thoughts and emotions that come up when we engage with others. Finally, using the body-speech-mind practice that is also introduced later in the book can provide us with the opportunity—in a group setting— to evoke both our connections and our obstacles to connection so that we can get to know them well.

Doesn't it seem like it takes a lot of work to simply be?

3
Sitting Meditation

IN THE CONTEMPLATIVE APPROACH to working with others, the foundation practice by which we become thoroughly acquainted with ourselves is the sitting practice of mindfulness-awareness meditation. The practice of meditation provides us with a regular opportunity to examine our experience, to make friends with ourselves, and to reconnect with our brilliant sanity. In meditation practice, we sit down and see for ourselves what our experience is. It is quite rare for any of us in the West to take the time to simply sit down with ourselves in this way.

We might think that to take time to "do nothing" like this is selfish or even pointless. Yet it is by sitting quietly, doing very little, that we discover within ourselves the resources that enable us to be genuinely helpful to others. As we have seen, we spend a great deal of time not being present with what is happening. The sitting practice of meditation helps us become less distracted, more present. It helps us cultivate awareness that lets us recognize the difference between being present and not being present. Sometimes this is called taming the mind.

There is a traditional analogy that compares our minds to a wild horse. Imagine a beautiful, spirited wild horse, running freely over the plains, jumping and prancing with delight, its mane flowing and its tail dancing. If we want to tame the horse so that we can ride it, we might think that the thing to do is to put it in a small, enclosed place. But that doesn't tame the horse. Even if we could then ride it, all we would have done is to break its spirit. We tend to do this with our minds. We think that we can rein ourselves in, keep a watch on all that we do—give ourselves very little rope. We think, for example, "I had better keep a close watch on myself so I don't do anything dumb." Or we might try to control how we feel: "I won't let myself feel upset now. In fact, I don't ever want to feel that." This kind of approach doesn't lead to the discovery of our brilliant sanity—it just makes us tense and rigid and filled with self-doubt.

Would it then be better to let the horse run free and not try to restrict it at all? If we do that the horse will probably run off wherever it wants and we will never come to ride it. We try this too with our minds. We just give up on developing any consistency or discipline: "I think I'll just watch a video and maybe start meditation practice next year." Or: "I don't need to do anything special. I can see what I'm doing without something artificial like meditation." When left to run free, our minds stay just as distracted as ever and we cultivate neither our ability to be present nor our recognition of our brilliant sanity.

There is another way. Instead of being too restrictive or not trying at all, we can put our horse into a big roomy pasture, with lots of space in which to dance and run, but we can put a fence around this big place. Then the horse can start to settle down and we can gradually approach it and make friends. We can come to ride the horse without breaking its magnificent spiritedness.

Sitting meditation is like providing our wild-horse minds with a big pasture with a fence around it. The fence is the technique of meditation itself. This kind of meditation is about discovering who we are as ordinary human beings. Being ordinary here means to start to recognize our true nature—brilliant sanity. This kind of meditation is about seeing who we are already, not about changing ourselves into higher beings, celestial beings, or anything else. It is not a kind of aerobics of the mind in which we give our minds a workout so that they will finally relax from exhaustion. Nor is it a way of tuning into an extraordinary state of consciousness. By sitting down and being interested in who we are we begin to express the very qualities of our sanity: openness, curiosity, and gentleness.

We can approach our practice with an attitude of open-mindedness. Our intention can be to see what we see, experience what we experience, without prejudice. Openness means that if our practice is blissfully wonderful, we let it be that way. If it is fraught with painful emotions, we let it be that way. There is room in our minds for whatever comes. Our practice does not have to be any way in particular. There is no wrong experience in meditation.

Along with openness, we can aspire to be curious. We are interested in what arises, not in the sense of trying to figure it out or to trace back where a particular thought or image came from, but just interested enough to notice thoughts, feel emotions, recognize perceptions. Rather than turning to books or experts to tell us who we are, we can look for ourselves.

Compassion and gentleness are also very important. We all have a tendency to judge our experience. Many of us are especially good at judging our experiences negatively. So in our meditation practice, we can practice treating ourselves gently, kindly. When we notice that we are lost in thought and are not using the meditation technique at all, we can softly, gently, bring ourselves back to the technique. Our willingness to sit down with ourselves is an expression of friendliness to ourselves. We are already saying something like, I'm worthy of spending time with.

The Technique

The technique of mindfulness-awareness sitting practice has three aspects: body, breath, and thoughts.

Body. First, we pay attention to posture. Generally, as we did in the mall practice in the previous chapter, it is important to take an upright but relaxed posture. Traditionally this is done by sitting on a cushion on the floor. At Naropa we sit on boxy cushions called *gomden*s. These are quite firm and high enough for the legs to rest in front without any extra weight on them. Some people prefer *zafu*s, round cushions that are Japanese in origin. Both the gomden and zafu are usually placed on a padded mat called a *zabuton*. If you don't have a cushion, you can fold up a blanket. If our seats are squishy or wobbly it is harder to sit for any length of time. Also, if they are not wide enough we will feel like we are going to tip over. We won't feel grounded on the earth, and sitting practice is about being on the earth.

If you can't sit on the floor because of physical limitations of one sort or another, sit on a chair. As with the cushions, it is best to choose a chair that is firm but not painfully hard. It is good if the seat is flat—not inclined toward the back with the knees higher than the hips. We want to be able to sit with our backs straight. It takes some looking around to find a chair that will let us do this.

Once we have chosen our seats, we sit down. If we are on a cushion, we loosely cross our legs in front of us. It is easier on the back to let the knees be up, not trying to force them to the floor. Some traditions say that the full lotus posture, with the feet resting on the thighs, is the best and most stable posture, but it is not necessary here. We are trying to find a balance that is both straight and relaxed. So, we just sit down and cross our legs in front of us.

If you are sitting in a chair, place your feet on the floor so that they are carrying a little weight. You may have to put something under your feet to do this if you are short like me.

Then, whether we are sitting on a cushion or on a chair, we let our backs rise from the stable seat we have created. The head and shoulders are upright and squared to the front. Tuck the chin in just a little and let the mouth be relaxed. Rest the hands on the thighs. If we let our arms hang down naturally and then place our hands on our thighs, our arms will be alongside our bodies.

Sometimes this posture is described as regal. The idea is that the posture reflects our brilliant sanity, our basic, inherent dignity. It is relaxed and upright, not rigid and uptight.

The eyes are open in this practice. Some meditative techniques are designed to foster relaxation or to distract us from the demands of the world. This practice is designed to help us be more present and awake, so we leave the eyes open. Also, we are preparing ourselves to be present in the world, so we practice by including the environment, not shutting it out. The gaze is downward, about six feet in front of us. It is not a strained gaze like looking down at our feet, nor is it totally unrestrained. We are always trying to find a balance, so we begin with the gaze close, but not too close. Our focus is either clear or soft, it doesn't matter. The idea is that whatever is in front of us is what is in front of us. We are not staring at what is there, but rather simply letting it be.

When we first sit down to begin our practice, the first thing we do is take the posture. Then, we take a moment to be in the environment. We acknowledge where we are, recognize the space, the room, within which we are going to practice. If you are new to practice, it is good to just hold the posture for a few minutes and see what that is like.

If at any point you feel physically very uncomfortable, take a moment to readjust your posture. You might trade which leg is on the bottom or sit up more straight. Just do this very simply without making a big deal. If you find that you are doing this a lot, you might need to make some changes in your setup. If you are very long legged, make sure that you are sitting up high enough so that your hips are above your knees. It may take more than one cushion or blanket. If you are short legged, the opposite may apply. Don't sit so high that your legs have no weight on them. Experiment and find what works for you. A bit of knee pain or a sore back are common when one is beginning. Your body will settle down and only minor aches will come and go. Try not to let the search for the perfect cushion replace the heart of your practice!

Breath. Next is working with the breath. Many meditative traditions use the breath as a reference point. Breathing happens in the present moment, so if our attention is with the breath, we are anchored in what is now. We use the breath because it is available and neutral. There is no idea here that breath is special in some way; there is no special breathing used. Whatever our breathing is like, right at this moment, we let it be that way. If our breathing is shallow and quick or if it is deep and slow, it doesn't matter. This technique is about seeing what is happening. If we change our breathing, we'll only see what we've changed, not what is happening.

We place the attention lightly on the breath. Sometimes this is quantified as 25 percent of the attention on the breath. This is a guideline so we won't get too heavy handed or overly earnest about what we are doing. The rest of our attention is on body and environment.

Some traditions use both the inbreath and the outbreath. In this technique we pay attention especially to the outbreath. When breath goes out, we go out along with it. I have found that I get more questions about what that means than about anything else connected with the practice. To go out with our breath means that our minds, our attention, goes out with the breath. We don't imagine the breath or visualize anything. We just let mind and attention go out as breath goes out. Then, the breath dissolves and the attention we have placed on it dissolves too. Since we are not separate from our minds, we can say that as our attention dissolves, we dissolve. Breath goes out; we go out. This going out is related to our intention to go out toward others and so this technique is a particularly good one for aspiring helpers.

Breath goes out and then there is a gap. There are no special instructions for what to do during the inbreath. There is a rhythm between having something to do—going out with the breath—and not having something in particular to do, the inbreath.

As you did with the posture, if you are new to practice, it is good to spend a few minutes just working with the breath. That is the second part of the technique.

Thoughts. The third part of the technique has to do with what you probably noticed when you worked with the breathing. Even though you intend to go out with your outbreath, be with your outbreath, you find that you get distracted. You might get more or less lost in thought or get caught up in a body sensation or an emotion. In any case, you are no longer going out with your breath. This does not mean that you are no longer doing the technique. We are, after all, interested in what we are and what we do. Getting distracted is part of who and what we are. In this technique we acknowledge that we are distracted by using the label "thinking." We silently say "thinking" to ourselves as a way of recognizing what has just happened. Then we return to working with the breath. This is where gentleness is important. Labeling thinking does not mean, You idiot, you were thinking and you should be following your breath. It just means that thinking just happened. In this technique we regard all distractions as thinking. As you may have seen in the exercises in the last chapter, our minds are very much part of our experience of our perceptions and our emotions, so we say "thinking" to cover all the things we do that take us away from the present moment.

We also use "thinking" to cover all kinds of thoughts. It doesn't matter at all what you were thinking or for how long. If you got lost in a juicy fantasy about a hot fudge sundae or if you had a momentary excursion into your budget or if you thought of maiming your neighbor whose dog poops on your lawn—it all gets labeled "thinking" for the purposes of this practice.

We don't have to label every little flicker of thought that arises. We can save the label for when we get caught up or lost. I had a meditation instructor once tell me, "You don't have to use labeling like a cleanser." We can trust that we will know what's a big enough distraction to label. Otherwise we might end up saying "thinking . . . thinking . . . thinking" the whole time!

Summary of the Technique

That's the technique. It is very simple. It is also quite thorough in revealing us to ourselves. In that way it can also be difficult. It is important to remember that we are applying our openness, curiosity, and gentleness when we meditate. At the same time, if you get caught up in judging your practice or not being open or curious, just label it "thinking" when you notice. It is not necessary to analyze any further. Just gently return to the technique.

If, at any point during your practice, you get all mixed up, you can make a fresh start. If you are following your thoughts and labeling your breath, or if you are so confused that you don't have a clue what you're doing, just stop. Start over.

Readjust your posture, look around the room, and come back into the environment. Then once again begin to work with your breath, go out with the outbreath. When you get distracted, label your thoughts as thinking.

To restate briefly: There are three aspects to the technique. Take a good posture, go out with the breath, label thoughts as thinking.

The sitting practice of mindfulness-awareness meditation is particularly helpful for connecting us to both the emptiness and the fullness aspects of our minds. Sitting silently with ourselves gives us the opportunity to experience space and what arises in it. From the point of view of practice, whatever arises, arises. It comes and it goes. If we get caught up in it and we recognize it, we label it "thinking." We don't say good thought or bad thought. We just say "thinking," and go out with the outbreath. The practice is sometimes described as mixing mind and space, or mixing breath and space.

Other Details

How long should we practice? How often? Where? When you are beginning, it is good to practice for shorter periods. It may be tempting to take on long sitting blocks, but you might find that you become tired of practicing quite quickly. Everyone is different, so you can see what works for you, but in general, it is good to start gradually. Sit for perhaps twenty minutes or so and build up slowly to an hour.

As for how often, a daily practice is the best. Having continuity provides familiarity and ordinariness in meditation practice. Continuity makes it easier to keep going when practice becomes boring or when difficult experiences arise. Since it is sometimes more difficult to practice at the beginning, having a regular routine can be extremely helpful. Along with this, it is helpful to practice at the same time each day. For many people, this is the first thing in the morning. Again, there are individual differences. You will have to see for yourself.

In general, you want to practice in an environment that supports what you are doing. A quiet room with few distractions is good. Few people have a room they can devote just to meditation, so sometimes people create a corner of a room or an area in a larger space that they set aside for their practice. It is good to have what is in front of you be neutral or related to your practice. For example, you probably won't do well sitting in front of the television. Many people like to put sacred objects or pictures in front of them when they practice. Feel free to use things from your own tradition or culture. If they remind you of what you are doing or of your inspiration to help others, they're fine. If they provide lots of opportunities to drift off into internal dialogues and discussions, maybe not. Some people like to light candles and incense as reminders of the ever-changing quality of experience. They are not essential, but by all means use them if you like. Once again, it is up to you to see what feels workable.

Many find that sitting with a group is very supportive to their practice. If you live in an area where there is a meditation center that feels inviting to you, you might explore the possibility of joining their group meditation sessions.

Some Concerns for New and Old Meditators

Often new meditators make the mistake of thinking that we are trying to get rid of our thoughts. No. We are trying to see what we do and who we are. By the time you realize that you are thinking, you are already "back" on your cushion. The labeling just acknowledges what's been happening.

Another mistaken notion is to think that our practice should be some particular way—peaceful, wakeful, spiritual, whatever. Again, no. However your practice is, that's how it is. If you are making some effort to use the technique, then it is good practice. It doesn't matter in the least if you feel better or worse when you are done.

A story is often told of the Buddha being asked by a musician how tightly he should hold his mind when he practiced. Should he hold his mind tightly and catch every thought? Or should he let his mind be loose and perhaps miss most of what happened? The Buddha in turn asked him how he tuned his instrument. Did he make the strings tight or loose? The musician said that he tuned them not too tight and not too loose. It is the same in meditation, replied the Buddha.

No one can tell you when you are too tight or too loose in your practice. You have to experiment for yourself. In the same way that it is hard to tell someone else how hot to make your bath water, you have to find your own way in meditation practice.

If you intend to continue your meditation practice, at some point you will need to work with a meditation instructor who can help you fine tune it. We all fall into mistakes with our practice, usually the ones I've just mentioned. In the appendix of this book are listed centers where you can connect with a meditation instructor trained in this technique. At the same time, you might find that another tradition might be more compatible for you. That's fine too. The point is to investigate our experience for ourselves so that we become familiar with all the ins and outs of our own minds and are able to be present when another needs our help.

4
The Spectrum of Brilliant Sanity

HELPING HAS TO DO with uncovering brilliant sanity, nurturing it, removing the obstacles to it. In order to help others to recognize their basic healthiness, their brilliant sanity, we have to be able to identify it in ourselves. Traditionally brilliant sanity is described as appearing in five basic ways. These five, whose roots are found in the Tibetan Vajrayana tradition of Buddhism, are called wisdoms or styles of sanity.

Brilliant sanity is like the sun. Each of us is like a unique prism through which the light of the sun passes and is broken up into a spectrum of five colors, and each color is associated with one of the five styles of sanity. For each of us this display of colors is slightly different. While we all have all five wisdoms, each of us has them in different proportions. Knowing about each of these five helps us to see the sanity that is already present in ourselves and in others. Sometimes a wisdom shows up in a diluted or disguised form, yet we can learn to detect it even then.

When we have the idea of sanity as our reference point in working with others, we are better able to support their strengths and their development of confidence. Looking only at what is wrong tends to make people feel that they are only a bunch of problems. This serves to undermine their ability to take care of themselves and leads to a false view of themselves as inadequate or helpless. Rather than uncovering brilliant sanity, focusing only on what is wrong has a way of further covering it up.

Here is an exercise to highlight this problem. Think of someone you know well and with whom you have had some difficult times. First list all of the things that you find difficult about this person. Include things such as style of communication, appearance, how you feel when you are with them, decisions they have made, habits that they have, personal qualities. Let yourself really get into all the things about this person that cause you any difficulty. When you have finished, notice how you are feeling. How do you feel toward this person now? Many people report feeling something negative—for example, resentment, impatience, dislike, discouragement.

Now, list all of the things about this person that you appreciate. Put as much effort into this part as you did for the first part. Include the same areas: style of communication, appearance, how you feel when you are with them, decisions they have made, habits that they have, personal qualities. What do you feel after you have finished this part of the exercise? You might have more positive feelings toward the person: appreciation, liking, tolerance, or good humor.

As helpers we need to be able to work with problems, but we need to do more. We need to be able to recognize sanity. As a psychotherapist I often spend a great deal of time working with the obstacles to experiencing brilliant sanity in myself and in my clients. In the field of psychotherapy we have a great many assessment techniques that help us be precise about mental disorders and psychopathology. Knowing about the five styles of sanity gives us something quite different. It helps us recognize and appreciate sanity. We will look more closely at the obstacles to experiencing brilliant sanity and how to work with them in later chapters. First, let us look at how to recognize sanity.

Our approach begins with becoming familiar with brilliant sanity in its many guises. The five-colored display of brilliant sanity can help us see our present pain and distress in the larger context of our lives. This helps us to not reduce ourselves to our present problems. It also provides us with a basis for recognizing sanity and identifying resources in some places we might otherwise ignore. Our interest in sanity naturally leads to supporting the cultivation of curiosity, openness, and warmth in those we hope to help.

In this chapter we will also identify some examples of how the five wisdoms might look when they are clouded over or confused. In the next chapter, "Touch and Go," we will explore how we can work with these potential sources of sanity in order to reconnect with them again.

The Wisdom of Openness

The first kind of sanity is associated with the color white, which is like the absence of any color, any preferences. This kind of sanity is connected with open-mindedness and appreciation for immediate experience: whatever allows us to directly experience our own brilliant sanity and that of others with an attitude of sacredness or unfixated mind. This could include formal mindfulness practices and informal practices. In a later chapter we will examine how to help others develop mindfulness practices using their everyday experiences.

What do we and others regard as sacred? Where in our lives do we cultivate direct experience? Can we tell the difference between direct experience and concept? Most people have some areas where they can recognize this distinction.

My father was an avid golfer. We used to jokingly say that it was his religion. When I would talk to him about meditation, he understood a lot of what I had to say because it was similar to his experience playing golf. If he thought too much about how to hit a shot, he would get too tight and the ball might dribble a short distance or maybe sail off in the wrong direction. If he didn't try at all, the ball might go in the right direction, but not go far. If he relaxed his mind, letting the thoughts come and go without getting caught up in them, then he could bring together his body, mind, and knowledge and hit a really good shot. So he knew a lot about how to let distracting thoughts go.

We can become interested in when it is that we are open. For example, are we open to experiencing our sense perceptions—what we can see and hear and so on? Or do we turn away from things that we label as unpleasant, refusing to even experience them? For example, I know that I don't like eggplant. If I know there is eggplant in a dish, I wrinkle my nose and expect a bad taste. Recently I was quite surprised when I enjoyed a dish and then was told that it contained eggplant. Because of my attitude I had previously not really tasted the eggplant; I had only tasted my ideas about it.

Are we willing to feel all our feelings? Which ones can we welcome? I've known many women who can readily let themselves feel sad. But if they start to feel anger, it is so difficult and undesirable to them that they don't let themselves feel it. They turn it into body tension or even into depression. I've met many men who do just the opposite: anger is okay, but sadness is to be rejected as weak. These are patterns we have learned from growing up in a particular culture. We may find it easier to be open to some feelings than others. Those we are open to are opportunities to recognize our capacity for this kind of sanity.

How much of our body are we able to experience directly? Are there parts we are more in touch with than others? I remember once attending a workshop where the presenter described a posture he called "the hunch." This is the one where the pelvis is pulled back, and the head goes forward to compensate. He suggested that this posture came from not being willing to feel the genital area, not being willing to feel our sexuality. In someone who practices the hunch, we might find that there is more openness to what can be seen with the eyes than what can be felt in the loins.

When the sanity of openness is covered up it can manifest in the disguise of great stubbornness or a quality of thickness. When we feel slow, lazy, and stupid in some area of our life it indicates that we have lost touch with the wisdom of openness. For instance, we might find that we just cannot remember to go to the doctor for our checkup. Perhaps we are afraid of what we might be told. To maintain our ignorance, we forget our appointment.

The Wisdom of Appreciating the Richness of Experience

This kind of sanity, associated with the color of pure gold, has to do with recognizing our inherent riches, our resources. These can be material or psychological. What are our strengths? How much awareness do we have of them? When are we good caretakers? For others? For ourselves? Many people show a lot of generosity to others even when they don't to themselves.

When do we show genuine confidence? I once knew a student who was very quiet in class and only spoke if she was called on. She seemed quiet around her classmates even outside of class. Then I saw her at a dance. She was totally confident in her ability to express herself through movement. She was dazzling and entertaining. Her confidence manifested much more strongly in her body than in her speech.

In what areas are we tolerant of differences? Are we good at appreciating different ethnic groups? Or maybe just different ethnic foods?

In what areas do we appreciate ourselves? What do we already know about making friends with ourselves?

Appreciating the richness of experience includes anything in our world: materials, people, qualities. Being able to appreciate the accomplishments of others, for example, is a tremendous resource that can carry us past jealousy and pettiness. Do we have a particular appreciation for a well-written mystery? Are we especially grateful when we hear a beautifully played violin concerto?

How do we express our appreciation of sense perceptions? Through classical music? Painting? MTV? Are we appreciative of physical sensations? Lovemaking? Food? Are we appreciative of emotions? Which ones? Some people really enjoy feeling tenderhearted. They will say that a movie was great if it made them cry. Others—sky-divers, rock-climbers, horror-movie fans—really have a good time when they feel scared. They appreciate the feeling of aliveness that accompanies fear.

When the wisdom of appreciation is covered up it can leak out as a feeling of poverty or a sense that we are not worthwhile at all. It can also show up as the opposite of feeling bad about ourselves—as arrogance. Feeling as though we are not enough and acting as though we are a really big deal are both twists on this basic wisdom. They are signs that we have the potential for showing a good deal of appreciation even though we aren't right now.

The Wisdom of Clarity

The third kind of wisdom correlates with the sanity of developing our intellect, curiosity, and clarity. It is associated with the deep blue color of a clear sky. What do we get curious about? What topic is irresistible to us? How is it pursued? Do we, for example, dive right in whenever opera is brought up? Or politics? Or football?

I know a woman who is passionately interested in anything to do with the Mafia. At the drop of a hat she can start talking about its people, its customs, its history. She is like a child who is excited at the prospect of a new toy. Her enthusiastic curiosity leads her to read every new book on the subject, to watch every movie and documentary. Years ago she recognized a man on the street that the police had been looking for. This is clearly an area in which she has developed this kind of sanity.

In what ways do we cultivate the ability to think clearly? Do we think through the pros and cons of a project before we start it? Do we keep track of our finances? Do we utilize our analytical skills in our work?

In what areas do we expand our sense of how things work? I remember when I lived in a cottage on a lake some years ago. The pump for the very poor well kept breaking down. One day a friend was visiting when this happened. I was in the habit of calling the landlord and then getting upset when he took several days to getting around to fixing it. My friend, without a moment's hesitation, said, "Let's go look at it. Maybe we can figure it out." I was astounded. I had never been curious about machinery. I had always regarded it as semimagical. Sure enough, he looked at the pump and gave it a good clout, and it started right up. After that, I could get it going again myself. This friend was exercising the sanity of curiosity and inquisitiveness. (I, of course, had been practicing the opposite.)

If someone becomes a little more aware of how a particular pattern works, it is a reflection of this kind of sanity. If, for example, a young woman notices that she keeps choosing the same kind of unavailable men and then ending up in unsatisfactory relationships, she has begun to see how one event leads to the next. This can lead to making a different choice next time.

Sometimes alcoholics talk about the value in thinking through what would happen if they took a drink. Maybe it seems as though it would be glamorous and relaxing, but experience has shown that it leads to throwing up and being anything but glamorous. This kind of application of one's logical mind reflects the sanity of clarity.

Clarifying one's goals and intentions is also part of this kind of sanity. What are the aspirations and hopes that we have? What would we like to offer to ourselves and to others? What do we value? What religious, philosophical, or spiritual views do we hold?

Sometimes we feel really fed up with ourselves when we have not lived up to our own beliefs. Then we may feel a kind of self-disgust. If we can recognize the sanity within this kind of revulsion, as helpers we can support the clarity that sees through the previous self-deception or hypocrisy, and at the same time, not feed the tendency we all have to become self-aggressive when we discover our mistakes.

Working with and respecting boundaries can be part of this wisdom. Do we follow a schedule or have a routine? Can we get to appointments on time? Can we say no?

I once worked with a client learning how to set some limits with her adult daughters, who were imposing a whole slew of unreasonable demands on her. One day she called me at home. In the context of our relationship at the local mental health center, this was not allowed. I told her I couldn't talk to her on the phone and that if she felt she needed to talk, she should call the center's hotline. She hung up less than pleased with me. I wasn't feeling particularly comfortable either. But when we met again it turned out that this had been helpful to her after all. It had somehow shown her that it was possible to be clear and firm in setting limits. That week, she had for the first time said no to one of her daughters' demands.

Since this sanity involves the use of intellect, anything about which we have precise knowledge and understanding may reflect it. Do we know all the football standings? Can we recognize all the different birds in our state? Do we know how to figure out what is wrong when the car won't start? Can we explain how the tragedies of Shakespeare were a commentary on Elizabethan politics?

We have seen how revulsion and self-aggression can contain the seeds of this kind of wisdom. Anger, too, is often a sign that the wisdom of clarity exists as a potential in us. Usually when we get angry we are rejecting something that we don't like. First, though, we have to have had a clear glimpse of whatever it is we are rejecting!

The Wisdom of Compassion and Genuine Relationship

The fourth sanity is our capacity for genuine relationship. It is associated with warm, vibrant red. In what ways do we recognize our connection with others? In what ways do we seek to communicate with them? This sanity lies in our attempts to reach out to others. Genuine communication takes many different forms.

I know a couple who argue a lot. When I asked them once why they were always arguing, they both looked at me with astonishment. "Argue? We don't argue. We discuss things." They agreed on this. Clearly they were communicating just fine with each other. I was the one who had a problem.

In what situations do we express caring by listening? Many times this is the best way to express our connection with others. Do we listen to our employees? Our children? Our parents? Our partner? The lack of the willingness to listen is often the biggest obstacle in relationships. I know many families in which it is not easy to get in a word edgewise. What a gift it is for one of its members when someone is willing to sit down and simply listen to what he or she has to say!

This wisdom goes beyond simply caring or being nice. How do we show compassion? For example, maybe a criticizing mother is showing compassion for her child. Even though it seems as if she is being quite negative, criticizing and clamoring, when we really listen we find that she is exhorting her daughter not to let other teenagers talk her into doing something she doesn't want to do. Her style might lead to her message getting lost, but her intention to help her daughter is unselfish and genuine.

To what extent do we feel for others? Are we able to be with a friend who is grieving? Are we willing to experience the helplessness and sorrow that arises inside us as we keep her company?

Another way we are connected to others is through all of our formal relationships. How are we connected to others in clubs, organizations, or at work? To what extent are we a participant? A leader?

When we start looking we see how connected and interconnected we all are. Our ability to feel this connection and to interact with each other with genuine compassion and communication is this fourth sanity.

Confused expressions of this kind of sanity show up whenever we become demanding about relationships: when we become possessive and clinging. The desperate attempt to escape loneliness at all costs can lead us into unsatisfying and even dangerous relationships, yet it is a sign that we have this sanity hidden within us.

The Wisdom of Skillful Action

The last sanity is effective and compassionate action. It is associated with green, the color of growing plants and of traffic lights that tell us to go.

In seeking to recognize this sanity, we might ask ourselves, In what areas do we show efficiency and competence? How do we relate with work, both professional and domestic? Knowing how to do our job well is part of this sanity. Watching a fast-order cook can sometimes provide us with an example of the grace and elegance of efficient movement. The eggs and the potatoes get fried, the coffee is perked, and the toast doesn't get burned.

Getting the grocery shopping done, balancing the budget, remembering to pick up one child from a piano lesson and another from soccer practice without getting home too late to get dinner started requires this kind of competency.

A blind person who uses his hearing to determine what is happening is demonstrating this kind of sanity. Another person who uses the sense of sight to put together patchwork quilts is also.

How are we creative? Do we know how to use just a little money to make a welcoming home? Do we paint? Play a musical instrument? Write poetry? Make up silly songs?

And, of course, taking actions that are helpful to others expresses this kind of sanity.

When the wisdom of skillful action is clouded over it can become meaningless activity or speediness. It can take the form of mental speed in which our minds run wildly or obsessively over the same stories again and again. We might experience self-doubt or unrealistic fears. These kinds of experiences that cause us pain and do not really help anyone can contain within them the germ of this wisdom.

The Full Spectrum

It may be a combination of all five wisdoms that leads someone to read a book about how to be helpful. The willingness to try something new is the sanity of openness. Settling down and looking into our own resources is the wisdom of appreciation, and the curiosity to learn about how to do it is a sign of the wisdom of clarity. The desire to connect with others and help them reflects the wisdom of genuine relationship, and putting what we learn into practice requires skillful action.

It is not particularly important to figure out to which wisdom a particular experience or expression may belong. The point is that by looking at the whole array of sanity, we may notice aspects of our own or someone else's life that reflect sanity that we might otherwise overlook.

It is also important to notice sanity even though it may be quite distorted or disguised. We can't always tell just by looking at the surface of things. As with the argumentative couple and the critical mother above, when we are looking for sanity we have to exercise curiosity and go deeper than the surface of things. For example, a psychotic person who dreams of putting on a fabulous art show to make a lot of money to feed all the world's children is showing compassion, and maybe exertion. A woman who stays in an abusive relationship to keep food on the table for her children may be showing compassion too. Clearly, all of these examples can be investigated from the point of view of confusion as well as sanity. The psychotic person who dreams of the art show may not be able to attend to the small details of how to feed himself. The mother in an abusive relationship may be exposing herself and her children to danger.

Our interest in sanity naturally leads to supporting the cultivation of curiosity, openness, and warmth in those we hope to help. What we are trying to do is to recognize sanity. Then, we may or may not respond overtly. But if we are interested in sanity, it will carry over into what we find worth pursuing, what we show curiosity about, what we think is worthwhile. The people we aspire to help may start to recognize these things too. Our allegiance may move in the direction of cultivating brilliant sanity wherever it may lie.

Part Two

Appreciating the Richness of Experience

5
Touch and Go

IN SITTING PRACTICE we have the opportunity to settle down and to see all kinds of things about ourselves. We notice how sometimes we are quite relaxed and feel content to just sit. We notice how at other times we feel as though we're about to jump out of our skins. We notice that we get lost in thoughts. We spend long periods of time going over old memories or making up scenarios of how we'd like to act the next time we see our old boyfriend. Emotions come and go. Sometimes they seem to come and stay for long stretches. When pleasant emotions come we might not mind, we might even enjoy it.

We might have a juicy fantasy going in which we get to live happily ever after with a sexy, attractive partner. When more difficult emotions come, we might wish that we could do something to prevent their arising at all. When we find ourselves going over and over a problem, feeling obsessed and claustrophobic, we might wish that we could just cut off our heads!

The more we sit, the more we see what seeds of experience we have planted and how they have come to maturity. A good farmer will determine which parts of the harvest can be used for food, which seeds will be the best to plant next year, and what things should be put into the compost to enrich the soil later. Sitting practice is also a bit like this. It is not that we have to keep anything particularly, but we could have the attitude that everything is useful. We can develop mindfulness by bringing attentiveness to anything at all. By using a technique called touch and go we can deepen our sitting practice and make use of everything in our experience, just like a good farmer.

The Need for Touch and Go

When we are new to sitting practice, we may start to notice more of what goes on in our minds. Maybe we are sitting, doing our meditation practice, and we get caught up in a memory of something we said yesterday at a meeting. We start to feel a little hot under the collar as we recall, with embarrassment, our foolish words. Oh, how we wish we had said something else! What do we do in our practice when this happens?

We might be tempted to quickly say, "Thinking," to ourselves as a way of getting this feeling to go away. Quick labeling is like the movement of waterbugs that skitter across the tops of ponds on the surface tension of the water. They don't even seem to get their feet wet. Instead of contacting our experience, we barely notice what we are thinking or feeling and rush off to go out with our breath.

Or we might get lost in this juicy and awful feeling and begin to remember all the other times we've done something similar. We might start to tell ourselves how stupid and incompetent we are. We could really get it going! We sink so deeply into our feelings that we forget where we are and what we're doing. Neither of these has much mindfulness or awareness to it.

Learning to Use Touch and Go

Instead, we are taught that we can practice touch and go. This means that when a feeling or thought or sensation arises, we touch it—feel it completely. We can touch quite completely in a moment. It is like tasting an anchovy. We can taste the salty, pungent flavor in just a moment. We can do the same thing with whatever arises during our practice. Instead of skittering away, we touch. We move toward what is happening instead of trying to get away. Rather than rejecting our experience we show an interest in it.

Then, having touched, we let it go. We touch and then we go out with our outbreath. Going is a kind of relaxation; we loosen our grip on ourselves. We might find that there can be an unforced rhythm of touching and going, not unlike the in and out of our breath.

There are two main mistakes we can make with this technique. I call the first one "touch and grab." Instead of touching and going, we hang on. We think things over; we try to figure them out. We don't have to do that. Once we have touched, we can just let go. The other mistake I call, "go and go." In this one, we don't let ourselves touch at all. This is the skittering away already described.

From the point of view of meditation practice, there are no good thoughts, no bad thoughts, no good feelings, no bad feelings. Whatever comes, we just let it come. We touch or taste our experience. We let the texture of our experience be present. We don't have to judge it at all, we can just let it be what it is.

When we touch an experience and let it go, there is no guarantee about what will happen next. Quite possibly something similar may arise in the next moment. In that case, we just practice with it in the same way. Touch it, let it go. We may find when we practice this way that the exact same thing never comes up. We might see how each moment is new and fresh. On the other hand, many times when we touch completely, letting go seems to happen quite naturally. When we let ourselves feel the hot-collared discomfort of embarrassment and touch for a moment just exactly how we feel, we often find that the struggle to get rid of that discomfort subsides by itself. Then we may experience a glimpse of noneffort, a moment of peace.

When we practice with touch and go in our sitting practice, it tends to make our experience feel richer. There is more of a rub, maybe even some irritation. We get more of a sense of what it is to be alive.

Touch and go is an extremely valuable technique for all of us who aspire to be genuine helpers. It is a tool that we can use in our sitting practice, during our daily lives as we work with our own feelings and thoughts, and also when we work with others whom we'd like to help.

Working with Emotions

When we extend the practice of touch and go into the rest of our lives it gives us a powerful way of working with emotions. Usually, we relate to our emotions in one of two ways. Either we suppress them, pushing them down, or we act them out, expressing them mindlessly. Neither of these works very well.

Suppressing emotions. When we suppress our feelings, we barely let ourselves notice them before we push them out of our awareness. It's as though we've tried to close the door in the face of a door-to-door salesman. But, like some very insistent salespeople, our emotions are not so easily gotten rid of. They tend to show up as tension held in our muscles or in our dreams. Often they turn into feelings of anxiety or disquiet that we don't understand. Many times they seem to burst out again at the most inconvenient time.

A woman with whom I teach, Trudy, told me the following story. She was in the parking lot of a shopping mall one day and ran into a friend of hers who had been having treatments for breast cancer. The friend could be dying, and Trudy didn't want to get into that, so she was feeling a bit awkward and even a little frightened. She firmly pushed away her uneasiness and greeted her friend with a warm smile. They spoke of inconsequential matters. Then the friend said that she was hoping to try hang-gliding. This sounded like a cheerful topic and Trudy joined in with relief. Then it was time to go. "See you soon," said the friend. "If we're both alive!" chorused Trudy.

The very thing Trudy had tried to push away popped out anyhow. The same thing can happen when a small disagreement escalates into a major fight. The anger that has been arising and being pushed down suddenly explodes when the lid is taken off just a little bit. Instead of touching the anger or the fear, we barely touch and then we push down. This is not touch and go.

Mindlessly expressing emotions. The other strategy we tend to employ with emotions is to immediately express them or act on them. Many psychotherapies seem to encourage this approach. Popular wisdom, too, says to us, "Get it out!" When we deal with our emotions in this way we don't really feel them. We act as though expressing our emotions will make them go away. Ironically, this kind of mindless expression only feeds our emotions. When we feel angry and start raising our voice, we soon find ourselves starting to shout. We get hotter and hotter and more upset and angry. We end up saying things we later regret. We get carried away by our anger. We feel as though we have no control.

Bringing touch and go to emotions. Touch and go provides us with a different way of working with our emotions. When an emotion arises, we can feel it completely, and then we let it go. We can let go by working with the breath as we do in our sitting practice, or we can let go by coming back to the present moment, paying attention to what is happening on the spot. For example, we can pay attention to the environment and to our sense perceptions. Instead of slipping into a habit of getting lost in anger and in hateful fantasies, we can pay attention to how we feel in our body: Are we hot? Are we tight anywhere? What kinds of thoughts are we having? We can get interested in what we can see and hear. Can we still really see the person we are angry with? Do we still hear what is being said, or have we begun to get lost in the world inside our own minds?

When we bring curiosity to what is happening as emotions arise, we allow ourselves to touch and then to let go. We don't use our sense perceptions to distract us from what we are feeling, but rather to explore what it is like to feel this feeling right now. As we do this, we begin to recognize that our feelings are our own. Nobody inflicts them on us. Generally, we have a way of saying, "You make me so mad," as though another person has reached into our heart and placed the feeling of anger there. That's not really how it happens.

We can become experts on our own experience when we bring touch and go into our lives. We see that we get angry because of our own perceptions, our own preferences and desires. We want things to be the way we like them. When things don't go the way we want—and they rarely do!—we push away our experience.

Jack doesn't like to have anything but classical music play when he eats out in a restaurant. If jazz or soft rock is played, he can get very angry. He may stop paying attention to the other people at the table. He doesn't notice the taste of his food.

Jack made an interesting discovery. When he practiced touch and go with the sound of the hated music, he found that it was not as bad as he thought. He had gotten so caught up in his opinions that he really didn't hear the music properly. He also touched his sense of irritation and let that go. He found he was more present. He could let the irritation come and go without having to add anything more to it. He began to enjoy his evenings out and his food tasted better. Jack found that he could work with the situation by attending to his own experience. He did not have to get restaurant managers to change what they played or to boycott restaurants in the future.

In the contemplative approach we understand that we are responsible for how we work with our own minds, our own experiences. The first step in not being a nuisance is taking responsibility for ourselves. When we work with our emotions in this way we take responsibility for how we feel. This doesn't mean we should not feel how we feel. Rather, it means it is up to us to work with ourselves however we are.

So, the first thing we do with our experience of emotion—anger, sadness, jealousy, pride, dullness, whatever it is—is to feel it completely. We touch. When we touch, we acknowledge that this is how *we* feel right now. Someone else might feel quite differently in the same situation, but this is how we feel. Touch and go makes things *very personal*.

Reconnecting with vitality. The assumption behind suppressing and acting out is that our emotions are something of a nuisance, some kind of interference. In the contemplative approach we regard our emotions as part of our wisdom. Our emotions can be understood to be energy mixed together with a story we tell ourselves. The energy itself, the sense of vitality we feel in our emotions, is a manifestation of our brilliant sanity. But we add to them a story about what we like and don't like.

For example, if we're interested in what jealousy really feels like and start to see how the story we tell ourselves is just thinking, we realize that we can be with the jealousy. Perhaps there is a cold feeling in the belly and heat on the back of the neck. Maybe the heart starts to race. We notice that we are having thoughts of wanting to hurt someone or telling ourselves that we are unattractive. We may spin out an elaborate tale of how other people are happy and we are not. Yet, we don't have to do anything to make it go away. We can touch the feelings and thoughts for a moment and really feel what they are like. We don't have to be dragged around by our feelings. We can choose to bring mindfulness to them. When we see that the thoughts are just thoughts, then the energy being appropriated by the jealous thinking is available to us. The sense of vitality that has been lost in the jealous story line is freed up. At the same time we can touch the softness of our hearts. We can be vulnerable because we have less to protect. We do not have to spend our time avoiding how we feel.

Every time we can practice touch and go, we open up our hearts. We stop trying to be different, we stop struggling for a moment. When we open to ourselves in this way, it also lets there be room for others. When we let there be room for ourselves and also for others, emotions start to shift. They stop being such a problem. Instead, they become a source of wealth. The clouds that have obscured our brilliant sanity begin to part, and our hidden sanity can emerge.

The emotions are powerful reminders to wake up and be present. They also contain tremendous energy, lots of vitality. When we are not trying to get them to go away, they give us back our own strengths.

Having let ourselves feel the texture and grit of our experience, we are more available to what is happening. We can then decide what to do next. The situation has become open. We might decide to say something, perhaps quietly, perhaps forcefully. We might talk to the manager of the restaurant and tell him that we do not like the music or ask him to turn it down. We might decide that we don't need to say anything at all. There is no prescription that we can apply to all situations. The idea is that we can access our own sanity and intelligence better when we are not using half or more of our energy in trying to not feel what we feel.

As we will see in later chapters, touch and go is a tool that we can use as we offer help to others. First, we practice it on the cushion; then we let it come into the rest of our lives. When we work in this way, we can bring mindfulness and the possibility of openness to any situation.

6
No Strings Attached

THE MORE WE PRACTICE SITTING MEDITATION, the more we become familiar with ourselves. We see many things about ourselves that we may have always known and many that we never knew. Often we are surprised to find how much of the time we are not present. Many people are quite astonished to discover how confused they are! Sometimes it seems that meditation has made us more confused than ever. Generally, though, we are just seeing how absent or confused we have been for a long time. It is easy, when we see such things in ourselves, to fall into a pattern of judging our experience.

"I like how I feel when I'm relaxed and peaceful."

"I hate how I feel when I'm impatient with my kids."

From there it is hardly even a small jump to, "I like *myself* when I'm relaxed and peaceful." "I don't like myself when I'm impatient."

The contemplative approach teaches us that when we reject ourselves, we create fertile soil in which the seeds of self-aggression and mindlessness flourish. These, in turn, can flower into a garden of misery in which we then live and that others enter when they encounter us. We have all spent time in such gardens. When we are in that kind of space we feel unlovable, unlikable, and hopeless. It is not a way that any of us would choose to be.

On the other hand, when we begin to cultivate *maitri*—loving-kindness—toward our own experience, we plant the seeds of openness and warmth not only toward ourselves but also toward others.

Self-Aggression

Sometimes when we practice meditation, we become acutely aware of ways in which we are unkind to ourselves and to others. The good news is that our mindfulness is increasing, and it is becoming more difficult to hide our less attractive habits from ourselves. Mindfulness as we have discussed it refers to a particular kind of clarity, a precise attentiveness to the details of our experience.

Sometimes a feeling of revulsion can arise when we see clearly how we are behaving mindlessly and without compassion. Quite possibly we might react to such clear insight by becoming self-aggressive, giving ourselves a hard time and creating a lot of guilt and obligation about what we ought to be doing: I shouldn't be doing this. I should be practicing more. I should be completely perfectly aware all the time. I should be this, that, or the other thing. And that's self-aggression. It is self-aggression because we are rejecting who and how we are in this moment. When I use the word "aggression" I mean that we are pushing away and rejecting something.

Other times we find that we feel strong negative emotions: anger, jealousy, envy, fear. The more we are able to practice touch and go when we sit, the more the highly textured nature of our experience will become clear. These textures and feelings may not fit with our ideas about what it means to be a good and helpful person, and we may be tempted to push them away. We may become aggressive toward these emotions.

Maitri—loving-kindness—is the opposite of aggression. In contemplative psychotherapy we use this word to refer specifically to tenderness and gentleness toward our own experience, whatever that experience is. We also call it "unconditional friendliness." In the West, especially, people need to develop maitri. For some reason—not genetically, but culturally—we're particularly prone to becoming self-aggressive. It just seems to be what we do. We get very ambitious, speedy, and aggressive toward ourselves, which is why it's so important for us to develop maitri—kindness toward our own experience.

Conditional Friendliness

Usually we have a lot of strings attached to our willingness to be friendly toward ourselves. We feel good about ourselves if we exercise every day, if we meditate "perfectly"—catching our thoughts every time, going out with every outbreath—if we eat the right foods, if our house is clean, if we are kind to our parents and children. We could become very extreme about this. We feel worthy of regarding ourselves with gentleness when we do what we think we're supposed to do—all of those "shoulds." We should resist falling into mindlessness; we should never overindulge; we should say yes to the right things and no to the wrong things. On the other hand, we tend to give ourselves a hard time when we don't live up to the shoulds. We overindulge and we wake up with our mind full of recriminations and we vow to do better.

This way of approaching ourselves is rooted in the idea that we have to watch ourselves really carefully. Otherwise, we'll do something else really dreadful. All of this is based on a notion of ourselves as really not very reliable, not very kind, and not very good.

We believe we're bad because of unkind things we've said or done. We're too fat or too thin. We're too obsessive, too codependent, not compassionate, lacking maitri. We think we should be further along than we are. "I've been practicing for a year now and I shouldn't be this neurotic," we say to ourselves. "I've been practicing twenty years now and I certainly shouldn't be this neurotic." When we say it out loud it's obviously ridiculous—but we really do drive ourselves with this kind of thing.

Maitri

Instead we could bring an attitude of maitri, an attitude of friendliness and gentleness, toward our experience. We can see it for what it is, which is the quality of mindfulness. And we can let it be what it is without giving ourselves a hard time, which is the quality of maitri. This may make maitri sound a bit like a fairy tale filled with cute fuzzy animals with large brown eyes and long eyelashes. Maybe even a bit cloyingly sweet. But that is not what maitri is.

It is very easy to use the term "maitri" incorrectly because we're all so gifted at twisting things to our own egocentric purposes. Maitri is not particularly patting ourselves on the back. But it's also not beating ourselves over the head. Maitri also does not mean what we sometimes see in popular psychology, "I'm okay, you're okay." "I'll ignore your neurosis if you'll ignore mine." The problem with that approach is that, unless it's based on something more than the desire to be nice, it tends to fall apart very quickly. And it's filled with self-deception.

Something else maitri does not mean is making excuses for ourselves. This is very important. When we act aggressively or unkindly, it is not loving-kindness to say to ourselves, "There, there, you had a good reason. It's okay. You did the best you could and if somebody got hurt, well, that's really a shame. But you couldn't help it." That's kind of a little pep talk we're giving ourselves in the locker room. It's a rationalization. Maitri is not that, not a way to avoid being responsible for our behavior. It's not a trick for letting things be all right that we know perfectly well are harmful.

In fact, maitri is not about words at all. It's not a thought that we have. It's a quality of our experience—a quality of gentleness. To begin with, we'll use some words to remind ourselves about it. But maitri itself is really more of an attitude, more of an experience, a softness and gentleness in our experience. It's not a thought or a judgment.

Maitri is not even particularly about liking ourselves, which is really just a judgment, another condition. Maitri is more about seeing clearly and letting be. We could use the word acceptance, not in the sense of judging something as acceptable, but rather, in the sense that we simply see what's happening. It is, perhaps, akin to forgiveness. When we forgive ourselves or someone else, it does not mean that we approve of what has been done. In fact, if we were condoning something, the question of forgiveness would not have to arise. To accept is to see clearly and still have an attitude of warmth.

A key point is that maitri is not based on ego. Ego, as we will explore more thoroughly in the next part, is the tendency to have a fixed and solid reference point about who we are. It's really the biggest condition of all. It is the attempt to narrow down who we are into a solid and unchanging self. It is based on rejecting who we really are, and it is the opposite of maitri.

Maitri is being gentle with who we are in any one moment—whoever we are right now. We can let ourselves be who we are right now, we don't have to pretend to be somebody else. Who we are is just fine. We can trust in our brilliant sanity.

Finally, to return to what is not maitri: it is not a technique. Maitri is not something that you can just apply like ointment on a sore. We can remind ourselves, "You know, I could have more maitri right now." And maybe we'll take a deep breath and be more gently present. But it's not a technique in the same way that sitting practice is a technique—where there's an actual form and something to do. With maitri there's nothing particular to do.

Maitri brings an attitude of friendliness, acceptance, and nonjudgmentalness to all of the aspects of our experience. It means we let ourselves see what is happening with us and we let it be whatever it is. It is a fundamentally welcoming attitude. We may make some choices about whether we will change our behavior in a particular instance, but first we need to let things be what they are so we can see them clearly. When we push experience away we tend to act without enough knowledge, and we also tend to act without compassion. How can we act skillfully when we are busy pushing away and thus not seeing what it is we want to change? Being able to make good and helpful choices depends on freeing ourselves from self-aggression.

7
Friendliness without Limit

As we have seen, maitri is unconditional gentleness and loving-kindness toward our experience. We begin by starting to develop maitri ourselves and then it naturally extends out as compassion toward others. This friendliness without limit is part of our brilliant sanity.

A friend to whom we can show only our very best behavior is not a real, genuine friend. Friends are the people we don't have to lie to or try to impress. They won't run screaming into the sunset when they see that really we have a problem with this or that we get angry about that. They might not like everything, but they're still friendly toward us and appreciate us and are concerned about our well-being and all those things we think friends should be. They might not approve of everything we do, and at the same time they don't necessarily pretend not to see it.

Unconditional friendliness is looking at our experience with the same kind of honesty that we hope to show to a genuine friend. We see all the warts and all the bumps and all the flaws—all of whatever is going on. We notice the unpleasant emotions and the pleasant emotions, the disagreeable and the agreeable sensations, the aggressive thoughts and the nonaggressive thoughts, and the unskillful and the skillful actions. Whatever it is. We see the tendency not to look. We see that we've been daydreaming and now we're not. Whatever comes up, we notice it. That's the mindfulness part of it. And then beyond that we regard it with gentleness. We don't push anything away as unworthy of being noticed. Maitri is related to the notion of self-respect. We can appreciate ourselves and have respect for our experience.

One of my friends had a difficult time when she was sitting during a meditation program. She was caught up in angry thoughts and could not drop them. She was worried about what other people thought of her. She went around and around within a dense labyrinth of negative thoughts about herself. Then, tea break came. She was so distraught that she was afraid to go out and mingle with the other people even though it was a day when silence was being practiced and she wouldn't even have to talk to anyone. So, she sat slumped over on her cushion as the others filed out. About ten minutes passed. A woman on the staff came in with a cup of tea for her. Very gently this woman handed my friend the tea and smiled at her. My friend started to weep. The staff member's smile and the cup of tea reminded her that she was not a bad person and a small window opened in her mind in which she could see what she had been doing and just let it be. She relaxed for a moment and the whirlwind of thoughts was revealed to be as empty as the wind. For a moment she stopped struggling to get herself to be different. That's maitri.

Cultivating Maitri through Mindfulness Practice

How is this quality cultivated? The first step in the cultivation of maitri is working with mindfulness. It's hard to bring gentleness to something we're not aware of. So the first thing is working with our mindfulness-awareness practice—seeing what arises, touching it, and letting it go. As we see more and more clearly, one of the things we see is our lack of gentleness. We also see that the lack of gentleness perpetuates our suffering. So mindfulness leads us to really recognize the need for gentleness. That's one thing that it does.

Another thing we learn from our sitting practice is not to grasp so tightly. We start to see how much we try to hang on to all kinds of things: who we wish we were, things that we want, relationships we wish we had or have and are afraid to lose. We can start to loosen up that quality of grasping a little bit. Simply seeing the grasping actually starts to loosen it up. As we do this, we begin to develop more of an attitude of nonaggression and gentleness. We feel the texture of our experience more and more directly because we're not grasping onto some things and pushing away others.

This approach leads to fearlessness. Being able to look at our own experience with honesty and gentleness is not easy. We have a lifetime of habits of turning away from the parts of our experience that are difficult or ugly. When painful memories arise we may have a habit of pushing them away. As we remember the foolish way we behaved yesterday, we may not want to feel embarrassed and so we quickly push the memory aside or get lost in a fantasy of how we could have done things differently. Instead of cultivating mindfulness and maitri we end up cultivating ignorance. Ironically, one of the things we might discover is that starting to allow ourselves to be present with painful feelings and thoughts can bring to light some of our richest resources.

A woman who had been sexually abused as a child was my meditation student. She began having anxiety attacks while she was sitting. She would tremble, her heart would race, and she would become very afraid. To begin with, she didn't have any idea what she was so frightened about. She stayed with the technique of the practice. She let herself touch her experience and let it go. She tried to be welcoming to whatever came. As she did this she began to develop the confidence that she really could be with her fear and uncertainty. I was impressed by her courage.

It was a number of years later that she remembered being sexually abused as a child. Because she had practiced being with fear, she was able to remember and feel what came up with the memories. Like many survivors of abuse she was tempted to take responsibility for what had happened to her as a child. For many it is easier to feel responsible than to feel the helplessness and fear and rage that often arises with such memories. She brought a great deal of openness and curiosity to her experience of remembering. She was able to recognize quickly that she did not have to blame herself for her father's inappropriate behavior. At the same time she could acknowledge her understandable desire for affection, which she also recalled. She let herself experience both that yearning and also the sadness that accompanied it, yet this was not a reason to blame or condemn herself. I believe it was her mindfulness and maitri practice that allowed her such openness and lack of self-aggression.

This woman is now a practicing psychotherapist. Her willingness to feel the pain, anger, helplessness, and so on that arose for her has made her a tremendously useful helper to others with similar experiences. She brings great courage and warmth to her work. She is able to help others bring both mindfulness and maitri to what comes up for them as they explore the present implications of their past experiences with abuse.

Being able to experience more and more directly, as this woman did, leads more and more to fearlessness, which, in turn, leads to more ability to experience things directly. They work together—fearlessness and mindfulness. We realize that there is nothing in particular to be afraid of. We *can* be with our experience without any filters. We can do that. And that fearlessness leads us to maitri.

Taking a Gradual Approach

A word of warning may be appropriate here. Sometimes we think that since we can experience things directly, we *should* do so. It can be the practice of maitri to take things gradually. Pushing ourselves to experience everything we possibly can—even maitri—is really just being aggressive with ourselves. If the woman who remembered her childhood abuse had called up her father, the perpetrator, the second that she remembered, she would have been taking on more than she was ready for. She took other steps that led her to feel ready for such a conversation. For example, she chose to discuss her memories with a close friend and to let herself take some time to sort through her feelings. She practiced a lot and became familiar with the feelings that came and went during this period of her life. Eventually she spoke with her father and the conversation was a different one than might have happened earlier. It was still very difficult, but she did not have to freeze her heart again as she had before the memories had arisen. She was able to continue to bring maitri to her experience and this brought benefit to her and even to her father.

As we practice in that way, both on and off the cushion, the story lines we've got about being basically bad start to dissolve or start to be recognized for what they are—just stories. We begin to realize that we're actually not so bad. We discover that we're worthwhile, gentle people.

A young man I know was giving himself a hard time because he hadn't landed an impressive job. He had plenty of training and experience and was a likable, responsible person. When he first started to look at what was happening he felt like a failure. This was pretty unpleasant, but he stayed with it. What he discovered as he became more curious about what was getting in his way was that he was carrying an out-of-date story about how people get jobs. He realized that he believed that as a really capable person, he would be offered a job by someone. This would happen magically through some mysterious grapevine of people who had the power to offer him a position. When he recognized this belief he experienced a good deal of embarrassment and not a little relief. There was no shame in seeking out a job and letting others know he was in the market. His willingness to look closely at his own beliefs and to experience the accompanying unpleasant emotions gave him the freedom to pursue his interests.

To summarize, maitri is unconditional gentleness and friendliness toward our experience, whatever arises in it. It's cultivated through mindfulness and it's the expression of our brilliant sanity.

Using Tonglen Practice to Develop Maitri

In addition to our mindfulness-awareness sitting practice, we can also practice tonglen—sending and taking—as a way to develop courage, compassion, and maitri. Here we will present how to do tonglen practice as a way to develop maitri. In part four we will examine how to extend the practice so that it helps us become more genuinely compassionate, friendly without limit. Both tonglen and basic sitting practice help us become more fearless.

Tonglen—a Tibetan word which means sending and taking—helps us appreciate our richness in an unusual way. It lets us make use of the very things we would most like to ignore or get rid of. It's very ecological! Instead of regarding our unwanted thoughts and emotions as problems, we see through tonglen practice that they are the very things we share with everybody else.

"Little emotions" like my impatience with slow salesclerks, my petty jealousy when someone else is recognized and I am not, my irritation with my husband when he doesn't intuit what I'd like him to do—all of these are great fodder for tonglen practice. "Big" emotions like the grief I still feel at my father's death, my fear about my own death, the sorrow I feel when I hear of an earthquake in Japan, the uncertainty I feel about whether I can really help anyone—these too are what I have in common with many other people. They are part of what connects me to others.

In tonglen we work both with these uncomfortable feelings and also with our inspiration to be of help to others. Tonglen is a practice that ripens our hearts. All the juicy, smelly, negative thoughts and feelings we have are the rich compost that lets our hearts mature. First, we will look at how to practice tonglen so that we bring an open heart to our own experiences. Doing this lets our hearts naturally soften toward others as well. Later we will look at the full tonglen meditation that gives us the chance to practice extending our compassion out of ourselves as far as we can.

Generally, we practice tonglen in the context of our sitting practice. So, we sit for a while and then we begin tonglen. After we've done the tonglen practice, then we return to mindfulness-awareness practice and let our minds settle again.

Flashing on brilliant sanity. We begin our practice by flashing on brilliant sanity. We briefly remind ourselves of our desire to awaken our compassion and maitri. This first step is quite brief, just a few seconds. It might feel like an abrupt shift.

We can flash on any one of brilliant sanity's three main qualities: openness, clarity, or warmth. Some find they can readily connect with a sense of openness, a sense of there being lots and lots of room in their minds. Others find it easier to tune into the clarity of awareness itself. Still others remember brilliant sanity by letting their hearts open. Many of these people do so by thinking of someone who touches their tenderness. I sometimes begin tonglen practice by remembering my old dog, Molly, who died in my arms. Lately I've often begun by remembering my father's last moments. It is traditionally suggested that we think of our mother or whoever cared for us as a child. However we do it, we begin by remembering our inspiration to do this practice.

Establishing the texture. The second step is to establish the texture of the practice. As we breathe in, we imagine that we are breathing in the feeling of heat, heaviness, and claustrophobia. It is not important to have a visual image of this, but we can just have a sense of this quality that is like what we would find if we could distill all painful experiences down to a pure essence.

With each breath, we breathe in hot, heavy, and dense. We can feel as if we are taking it in through all the pores of our bodies, from every direction. Then on each outbreath, we breathe out cool, light, and bright. The idea is that we breathe out the essence of relief from suffering, the essence of sanity itself. It is like a cool drink of water when we are hot, dirty, and thirsty. Once again, we send out this texture through all the pores of our body. The second step of tonglen practice is to breathe in and out in this way until the sense of texture is established and we have connected our breathing with these two alternating qualities.

Getting specific. Then, the third step is to identify a particular feeling, thought, or situation that is real and difficult for us right now. We breathe in all of the thoughts, feelings, and sensations that go with that situation, thought, or feeling. When we say "breathe in" we could also say "feel completely." Say that we have been having a hard time with a colleague. On the in-breath we breathe in all the tension, hard feelings, resentment, and fear that accompany this situation. Then, on the outbreath, we breathe out to ourselves relief from the difficulties. In this instance, maybe we would breathe out to ourselves a sense of relaxation, peacefulness, and courage. Or we could let it become ventilated, mixed with the vast openness of brilliant sanity. We don't have to think it through, tonglen is more connected to our emotions than to our thoughts. We just breathe in and feel the pain of the situation and breathe out relief and sanity. We continue working with a particular situation until it begins to relax and dissolve. It is a bit like airing out a suitcase we've kept in the basement by opening it out in the sun.

If nothing readily comes to mind as a situation to begin with, we can start with whatever is true right now, including our difficulty in getting started. We can breathe in our feeling of frustration or our feeling of inadequacy. Then, we just continue from there.

Doing tonglen in this way gives us the opportunity to be generous with ourselves—something many of us do not do too often. It is a chance to cultivate maitri. We can try to breathe out to ourselves a genuine sense of kindness. For many people this is quite difficult. We might feel that we don't deserve such kindness or that it is indulgent of us to spend time this way. When we find such negative reactions arising, we can just include them in the tonglen practice by breathing them in. Then we can breathe out to ourselves a quality of genuine friendliness. We can remember that we don't have to make judgments about our experience; we don't have to like or dislike what happens. Instead, we can simply breathe in our own pain, touch it, feel it. Then, we can breathe out relief and kindness. As we discover our own obstacles to letting kindness come in, we may learn something not only about ourselves, but also about what prevents others from easily accepting help.

We can be as specific and concrete as we need to be. Pema Chödrön, a Western-born Buddhist nun, once described how a student of hers imagined breathing out a nice hot cup of coffee for herself. That was all she felt she had to offer, and so she did what she could.

In tonglen we breathe in both the petty and the important things. We discover the resources we have to offer to ourselves. Later we will extend this practice to generating genuine compassion for others. But first, let us learn to do for ourselves what we aspire to do for others.

Part Three

Seeing Clearly

8

With the Best of Intentions

A KIND OF CRYSTAL CLARITY can arise in our minds when we have begun to settle down and make friends with ourselves as described in part two. Now we can look at the basic ground of helping: our own intentions and our understandings. In this chapter we will look closely and discover what our intentions are as helpers. In the following chapters we will explore how confusion arises despite our brilliant sanity, and how we can reconnect with that brilliance through the gateway of confusion itself.

The longing to offer our compassion and assistance to others is part of our inherent brilliant sanity. When we look into our experience and identify our resources, we do indeed discover this longing. We find it arising as the tenderhearted desire to protect our children from harm. We see it when we extend a steadying hand to the elderly stranger who stumbles near us. We feel it in our pain when we hear of the brutal killings in Rwanda.

Sometimes this desire is camouflaged as irritation and frustration. When we listen to a friend who tells us how she is once again brokenhearted at the end of a love affair, we want to yell at her, "Why do you keep picking the same kind of irresponsible men if you want to have a long-term relationship?" Or we feel ready to tear our hair out when we see our boss getting increasingly enraged about a situation over which neither he nor we have any control. We want to say, "You don't have to keep doing this. Stop it, don't you see how you're only making yourself and everybody around you miserable?"

This frustration also comes from our compassion. We have some glimpse that the person does not have to suffer so. We want to make them stop it. We want to remove suffering when we see it, but our desire to remove suffering is mixed up with our desire to be comfortable and not bothered by others' pain.

Sometimes, when our intentions are confused in this way, we end up saying or doing something that makes the situation worse. We end up being a nuisance. Our friend feels pushed away and misunderstood if we seem to be suggesting that her heartbreak is her fault. Our boss may turn his anger on us. Instead of saying, "Thank you so much for your insight and advice," he might be more likely to bellow, "Who asked you anyway? I have enough trouble without you butting in with your advice!"

Other times, we may be hesitant to offer our help. We hold back when we could offer something of value. We see someone with whom we work but don't know very well sitting and weeping. We don't know what to do so we pretend we don't see him. Then, we feel awkward and tongue-tied the next time we run into him at the copy machine. We feel as if we missed an opportunity to have offered some comfort. We might even feel regret that we did not extend ourselves.

Holding Back

Let us look at what might be going on when we hold back. Then we will look at some common mistakes helpers make when their desire to help is based on confusion about their intentions.

In the West many of us believe that we should all be able to take care of things for ourselves. Being macho, being able to "take it," and never complaining are often regarded as virtues. It is difficult to ask for help if we feel that doing so is an admission of some kind of personal flaw or failure. Most clients seeking therapy feel that they should have been able to solve their own difficulties. It is good for us to be sensitive to this feeling in the people we hope to help.

The other side of this sensitivity is the hesitation we may feel as potential helpers. Psychological studies have shown that a person in trouble is more likely to receive assistance when there is only one other person around. The likelihood of receiving help goes down as the number of available people rises. We are all too likely to say to ourselves that our help is not needed—after all, someone would surely be helping by now if it were necessary. This is known as "diffusion of responsibility." One of the most well-known instances of people holding back from helping was the murder of Kitty Genovese on the streets of Queens, New York. Numerous neighbors heard her shouts for help, and yet no one even called the police.

Sometimes we hold back when we see others not stepping in. We tend to look to others for information about how we should act. Instead of assessing the situation for ourselves, we might just blindly follow the flock. For Kitty Genovese this tendency was fatal.

Sometimes we hold back because we don't want the inconvenience of getting involved. We might be afraid that we will somehow become responsible for what happens.

Sometimes we have legitimate concerns. We have obligations that we need to meet and we don't have time to stop and help in what doesn't look like a crisis. Other times, perhaps we know that a particular person prefers to be left alone and that to offer help would be an intrusion.

But more often than not we hold back out of some kind of

fear of being wrong or foolish. We don't like feeling uncertain and so we don't stop long enough to see if we could be helpful. We race over the uncertain feeling and then the moment is gone, the situation is past.

We hold back because we don't like how we feel when we don't know the right thing to do. We hesitate because we are afraid that we might feel a way that is somewhat uncomfortable: foolish, uncertain, mistaken. Suppose we go up to the weeping coworker and he says, "I don't need any help." Or, worse, suppose he weeps even harder and then we don't know how to respond?

We can go beyond this kind of fear. Because of our ongoing meditation practice and our willingness to practice touch and go, we can become more at home with feeling uncomfortable. It is quite possible to go ahead even though we don't feel strong and confident.

Talking with other psychotherapists, I find that many of us frequently experience not knowing what to do next. When I began this kind of work I hoped that the more I did it the more confident I would feel because I would know more and more what to do in particular situations. Although this has happened to some degree, it is not how I thought it would be. Confidence does not come from having learned the "right" things to do as though there were a recipe for what to add to the batter when a client says, "I feel depressed." Add a pinch of cognitive therapy and stir well. No, whatever confidence I feel comes from being able to hang out with not knowing what to do yet. The first step is always this willingness to be present. We cannot know what technique to apply until we have been open and interested—that is, uncertain—first.

Usually, I have to rest with the uncertainty for a while before I know what to say or do next. Often, I have a good idea of what might be useful. On the other hand, I might still be wrong and say something that is not quite accurate for the client. If I buy into the story that I should have all the answers I not only make it harder for me to offer help (after all, how often are any of us absolutely certain we know the right thing to do?) but I also abort the client's opportunity to be creative. My job isn't to have all the answers. Often the best thing I can do is help my clients find their own resources and put myself out of a job.

When we feel the urge to help and then hold back, it is always useful to be curious about what is going on. Sometimes we are refraining for good reasons. The situation may be dangerous in a way that would only put us in harm's way to no purpose if we jumped into it. But many times we hold back because of insubstantial fears. Instead of waiting until our fears go away, we could just bring them along. We could be awkward and uncertain and still be helpful.

Confused Intentions

On the other extreme from holding back is going ahead with confused intentions. There are two main kinds of confused intentions. The first one has to do with how we regard ourselves. We can call it therapeutic materialism. Like the ordinary materialism of wanting to accumulate possessions in order to build ourselves up, therapeutic materialism is the confused intention to be helpful so we can feel good about ourselves.

We might offer our help to someone who doesn't really need it just because we want to be seen as generous and caring. We might want to show off our knowledge. We want to be important.

Codependent relationships are a variation on this theme. In a codependent relationship one partner is the long-suffering patient one while the other partner is the one who is making a mess of their life. Often this second person is either abusive or addictive. The long-suffering, codependent partner tries everything to help. He or she may make lots of suggestions, seek professional help, and forgive lapses. The codependent partner is often seen by others as patient and good while the abuser or addict is seen as a real screw-up who doesn't deserve such an angelic partner.

There is, of course, some genuine caring and compassion happening in codependent relationships. On the other hand, the saintlike partner is often terrified of not having a relationship and may enjoy the positive image he or she has created.

When we fall into therapeutic materialism we lose track of our clarity. Instead of having the welfare of the other person in mind, we really have our own interest at heart. This can be quite subtle and is very hard to admit to ourselves.

The second kind of confused intention is related to the first and occurs when we try to get the other person to change. In contemplative psychotherapy we call this therapeutic aggression. This is not aggression that is therapeutic. It is aggression masquerading as therapy. You don't have to be a therapist to fall into this mistake.

"Therapeutic aggression" is trying to get someone to change so that *we,* as helpers, can feel better. It occurs when we feel dissatisfied with what is going on with the other person. For example, a counselor works with a woman who comes in each week complaining about her boss. It is painful for him to sit with the frustration and helplessness that the client is feeling. Instead of helping her explore her experience and reach her own decision, the counselor starts offering suggestions about how the client could look for a new job and find a more congenial boss. The motivation for these suggestions is the counselor's discomfort with the client's pain and his worry that he is a bad counselor since the client is not making any changes.

We may offer advice to a friend whose state of mind troubles us. Perhaps our friend is feeling anxious. We have a hard time being anxious ourselves, so we do everything we can think of to divert him. "Oh, come on, don't get so caught up with yourself! Let's go play basketball." Maybe if our friend can touch his anxiety, he might find that there is something to learn from it. Often anxiety is a thin veneer over deeper feelings, but he won't find out about them if we are urging him to busy distractions. If we can successfully distract him, we might even use his activity as evidence of how helpful we've been. "See, you were feeling lousy and now look at how productive you've been!" We think we're pretty hot stuff, but all we've done is make it harder for our friend to know what is really happening for him. We might even have prevented him from taking care of what he needed to be taking care of.

In these examples, our intentions were confused. We really did want to help, but we also wanted to feel good about ourselves as good helpers. When we get caught up in proving something to ourselves, we are not able to be present for the other person. The actions we take are bound to be somewhat off-target.

No one who works in the helping professions has avoided these pitfalls. They happen for all of us. When we discover that we've gotten caught up in therapeutic materialism or aggression or in unnecessarily holding back, we have a choice. We can steamroll over our discovery and keep doing what we've been doing, or we can stop. It is not easy to admit to ourselves or others that we've been so misguided. Completely pure intention is rare. We cannot wait until we are sure that our intentions are without the blemish of self-interest, but we can aspire to be mindful and to clarify our intentions.

When we have found ourselves acting on our mistaken intentions, we can give ourselves a hard time or we can practice maitri. We have a chance to practice touch and go. We can simply notice what happened and how we are feeling right now as we acknowledge our failure to be helpful. We do not have to manipulate it any further. When we practice in this way, instead of proving our ineptitude, our mistakes can soften our hearts and remind us that we really do want to benefit others. When we can admit our errors, it invites others to be more "human" as well.

9

If I'm Brilliantly Sane, Why Am I So Confused?

IF WE ARE BRILLIANTLY SANE, possessing innate openness, clarity, and compassion, then why don't we feel better? Why are we so often confused, depressed, or angry? Why do we get caught up in mixed intentions? Why, when we want to help, do we end up feeling worse than when we started and causing the other person more distress? In this chapter we will look at how we lose touch with our brilliant sanity.

We can understand the path of losing touch with our basic nature in three stages: shock, uncertainty, and conviction. This three-step logic is based in part on my study of Buddhism and also on my work with clients over the years and discussions with colleagues. As we will see in chapter 11, shock, uncertainty, and conviction are the very same stages we go through in reconnecting with our brilliant sanity. First, let's look at how this path can lead us to confusion and ignorance.

Shock

The first stage in losing track of our inherent wakefulness occurs when we are suddenly faced with the unexpected. Something fresh and new occurs, and our reaction to it is to feel stunned or shocked. We feel as though the ground had shifted under our feet. It is like a psychic earthquake.

Judy's boyfriend sits her down and says, "There's something I have to tell you." She feels her heart start to pound. "I think we should stop seeing each other." Now, she feels really thrown off balance. Her world is suddenly different. The world in which Sam is her boyfriend and in which they have plans for the future and in which everybody knows her as being in this relationship is no longer true. The feeling of shock comes as a contrast to what she had taken for granted.

The shock doesn't have to be particularly unpleasant. We have been preparing for a big examination. We have studied for weeks. Now, exam time has come and instead of being difficult, it is easy. We are surprised and realize we have wasted our time learning details that are not called for.

The Three Marks

What Buddhism calls the three marks of existence are aspects of our life that we generally would prefer to avoid noticing. The first of these is impermanence. When we look around, it is not difficult to see that everything in the world and in our experience is changing. The seasons change, plants grow and die, we live for a time and then die. Our thoughts, emotions, and sensations come and go. When we look for something that is unchanging, we cannot find anything, yet we usually live as if things will stay the same. The onset of menopause, the discovery of the first gray hair, the end of a relationship: when we recognize that things are indeed impermanent, we often experience it as a shock.

The second mark of existence is egolessness. We would like to think that we are the same person today that we were as a child. We act as though there is something in us that is always the same. Yet if we look carefully at our experience, it may be difficult to find anything solid. A traditional contemplation we can do is to ask ourselves, "Who am I?" This is a good exercise to try. Let the question arise for you over a period of about an hour. See what you find.

Usually, we try to answer this by naming our roles, such as, I'm a mother; I'm a psychologist; I'm a computer programmer. But our roles can change, so they're not who we are.

Or we try to answer with, I'm the one who sees the tree; I'm the one asking this question. This response is more subtle, but when we try to find the seer or the asker, what do we find?

Buddhism suggests that there is nothing corresponding to our sense of a self that is unchanging and solid. It also suggests that the self that we take to be separate from our environment and others is also not truly there. Where is the seer who is separate from the seen? Is the experience of seeing a tree happening in our head? Or out there where the tree is? Is it some place in the middle? When we taste a hot pepper, is the taste in the pepper or in our mouth? The Buddhist teachings suggest that there is no experiencer separate from the experience. Where is the line that divides the dancer from the dance?

We use the word "nonduality" to describe our recognition of the absence of this separation. When I teach a class, I look around at the students sitting in front of me. My experience in that moment includes my seeing and hearing of them. I am not separate from them. In the same way, they are looking at and listening to me. I am part of their experience right then. We are not separate, but we are not the same either. Even though we cannot find a separate self, we all have our unique experience. Paradoxically, we are connected, but we are also each alone.

When something causes us to recognize that we are not what we took ourselves to be, it can be shocking. A man is laid off from a job he has held for twenty years. He is bewildered; he doesn't know what to do with himself. A child's parents tell him they are going to get divorced. Who is he now?

The third mark of existence is suffering. We can never get everything in our life to be comfortable and pleasant. No one is happy all the time. We get our house the way we like it, and the pipes freeze and we're without water for four days. Things are always falling apart and coming together in inconvenient ways.

To be human is to have pain in our lives. Childbirth is painful. Sickness comes to us regardless of our age. We get colds or cancer. We break wrists and legs. If we live long enough we will grow old and suffer the pains of not being able to do what we used to do. We all die.

Our suffering is often the result of our struggling against how things are. Much of the pain we experience is caused when we try to avoid it. In America many people avoid their painful emotions, such as fear or sadness, by becoming very busy. Then, we feel the pain of rushing around all the time never feeling really present. Many people don't notice how distressed they are feeling until they come home at night. When they try to go to sleep and there is no longer the distraction of work or television, they find that they are restless, worried, or depressed. They toss and turn, unable to let go and fall asleep. Many people feel only half alive. Coming face to face with the reality of our pain can be a shock.

As we can see, recognizing any one of the three marks—impermanence, egolessness, and suffering—can provide a moment of sharp contrast, a shock. For a moment we see and feel things just as they are. It may seem as though it happens *to* us, but close examination reveals that it is our own ignoring that has brought about the suddenness of the recognition. We prefer not to notice and so we become surprised.

Uncertainty

In the development of confusion the first stage, shock, is followed by uncertainty. We feel lost and bewildered. We don't know what to do or who we are. We might find ourselves starting in one direction and then abruptly going in another. An old friend of mine uses the word "scrambling" to describe this kind of activity. It is epitomized by jumping in our car and quickly driving off with no destination in mind. Most of us have done that or something like it.

Not knowing what to do or how to be, we start feeling frightened. We feel groundless and disoriented. We might feel afraid that we are losing our grip, going out of control, becoming crazy. Our tendency is to speed up. We try to get away from the feeling of uncertainty.

We may become lost in an avalanche of thoughts. We may run around generating errands and activities to fill all our time. There is a mounting sense of anxiety—which is much the same as feeling speedy in our minds. We are fearful, but we don't know what we are afraid of. Along with the mounting tension is a decreasing sense of body awareness. We lose track of simply being present. Instead of relying on our sense perceptions to orient us, we rely more and more on our thoughts. We replace direct experience with concepts.

On the path to developing confusion, we don't appreciate that the uncertainty contains sanity. We're more interested in trying to get away from any hint of it. Ironically, our attempt to escape uncertainty breeds still more of it: we get more and more out of touch and less and less certain.

I worked with a woman who spent a great deal of her time worrying. The more she worried, the less sure she became about what to do. She was so lost in her head that she didn't feel much in her body. Since she was not feeling her body, she had also lost touch with her emotions. When it came right down to it, she didn't know how she felt or what she really thought about anything. She was unsure because she had no real information. She wasn't present, so all she had was secondhand beliefs. Many people who get lost in their thoughts have a tremendous sense of vagueness and uncertainty.

Conviction

The third stage of developing confusion is called conviction. Since we are trying to get away from the uncomfortable feelings that brought the sense of shock, and we are also trying to escape from uncertainty, we are open to less and less of our actual experience. Our awareness becomes more and more narrow. There are fewer people we can be around, fewer places we can go, fewer feelings and thoughts that we will accommodate.

When we complete the journey to conviction, we often end up with a sense of staleness, stuckness. We feel vaguely unhappy or even severely depressed. We generally conclude that we are basically bad. Sometimes we conclude that everyone else is bad. Sometimes we even conclude both. We believe that we must be terrible people if we're feeling like this.

My experience in clinical practice and working with meditation students and with myself is that usually when we're giving ourselves a hard time, somewhere in us is the notion that we're basically bad—that we're not brilliantly sane and we're not basically good. We're basically pretty suspect. I've seen that at the base of every kind of psychopathology from neurosis to psychosis. It seems always to be there at the bottom.

Often this sense of badness takes the form of blaming. We blame ourselves and feel guilty and ashamed. Or we blame the government, or our job, or our upbringing. Many times this kind of conviction takes the form of holding strong opinions that we do not question. Or, it can take the form of a rigid belief in some kind of doctrine. Such a belief is not based on heartfelt understanding, but rather on fear of letting our minds and hearts be open.

We weave elaborate explanations, story lines that we use to

make sense of ourselves and our lives. But these stories are not based on our experience; they are based on guesswork and memory. For example, Jerry has a story line about why none of his relationships with women last more than a few weeks. "My mother was an alcoholic and she was really unreliable. So, it's hard for me to trust women. I need a caring and warm woman, and I can't find one anywhere." There may well be some truth that the seeds of Jerry's difficulty can be traced to his experience growing up with an alcoholic mother.

Some of our convictions have their seeds in childhood and often were formed even before we could speak. Generally, these early convictions, which we can carry into our adult lives without questioning them, are the best compromise we could have reached in order to survive in a less-than-perfect environment with less-than-perfect parents. In that sense, they were reflections of our sanity at the time. The problem, of course, is that we perpetuate them now when they are no longer appropriate or useful. In fact, they cause us great pain because we have developed patterns of cutting ourselves off from ourselves and others.

No matter how elaborate, story lines never tell the whole truth. We perpetuate them out of habit even when they have little relationship to our present lives. Jerry has not yet learned to be open to himself, so he avoids relationships that would require that of him. He chooses partners who will not be too demanding and then rejects them as uncaring. In this case, Jerry has concluded that others are bad: his mother, most women. It is not unusual for him to get caught up in feeling sorry for himself and sometimes wondering if there isn't something really terribly wrong with him.

Many people have a secret fear that they are fundamentally damaged, really messed up, missing a part. This is a conviction of one's own basic badness. Perhaps we all carry some variation of this belief at times. Whenever we lose track of maitri, this kind of self-aggression easily develops. Sometimes this hovering sense of badness is called low self-esteem. It is a feeling of worthlessness and lack of confidence that can become our constant companion. It is so pervasive that we don't really notice it. The end result is that our world becomes smaller, our minds become tighter, our sense perceptions become dulled. We have lost touch with our brilliant sanity.

We can go through these three stages in the flicker of an eyelash, or we might take quite a long time. At any moment we might be in different stages with respect to different situations. We might, for example, have reached the conviction that our mother was always mean to us and that is why we are distrustful. It has become an assumption that we no longer question. At the same time, we might in our relationship with a friend be in the midst of uncertainty and fearfulness.

When we have gone through all three stages—shock, uncertainty, and conviction—we end up relying on habitual patterns instead of making choices based on being present. We seek comfort in the familiar. We mindlessly choose to repeat past patterns of thought and behavior. Many times we find ourselves doing things that we don't enjoy simply because that's how we do it. We say things like, "I'm the kind of person who . . ." That's usually a sign that we're not present but are relying instead on a story line about ourselves.

The idea of change is frightening because we would have to open up and let in some vividness. We developed our habitual patterns to avoid the sharpness of direct experience, and we are not at all sure that we can face it.

How genuinely helpful are we capable of being if we are seeing the world through the filters of our distorted convictions? In the next chapter we will see how we maintain our sense of disconnection, but then we will take a look at how we can reverse these painful and damaging patterns.

10
The Light's On, but Nobody's Home

WE HAVE LOOKED at how the path of shock, uncertainty, and conviction can lead us to lose touch with our brilliant sanity. We end up feeling out of touch with ourselves and others, convinced of our own or others' unworkability or fearful of revealing too much of ourselves since we suspect we're basically not very good and probably pretty unlikable. These convictions are not true; they are based on ignoring what is really happening. Since they are our own fabrications, they are not very durable. They tend to fall apart all the time, and brilliant sanity has a way of popping up when we least expect it or feel like welcoming it.

Just as we've got a good flow of indignation going in support of a complaint about our partner, we suddenly remember that we didn't really tell him what we are now saying we did. We have a flash of sympathy for the very person we're so mad at. Our clarity and compassion are interfering with a really good argument. We were feeling so sure of ourselves!

Since brilliant sanity is our true nature, it shows up whenever we relax the story line that accompanies conviction. What do we do about this? How do we keep the message of our brilliant sanity and the three marks of existence from challenging whatever story line or version of ego we are currently clinging to? How do we keep uncertainty at bay?

The best way to keep ourselves from being too awake and inconvenienced—from the ego's point of view!—is to cultivate *mindlessness*. We all have habits and activities that help us to dull out, either a little bit or quite a lot. It is like driving in a winter snowstorm, unable to see clearly what is happening just in front of our car. We turn on the headlights and the light just bounces back at us. Our view is obscured and we tend to tighten up. In this chapter we will look at how we cultivate mindlessness. First, try the following short exercise.

Mindlessness

Sit down comfortably and practice mindfulness-awareness sitting for about five minutes. Then, instead of working with the technique to help you be more present and wakeful, do whatever you can to cultivate a sense of being absent and ignorant. Do this for another five minutes. Read this far, and then do the exercise.

Now, think back on what you did to cultivate mindlessness. What did you do with your body? your eyes? your posture? What did you do with your breathing? And what did you do with your mind?

I have asked many people to do this exercise. What we generally find is that we are all very good at becoming mindless. Some people let their bodies slump down, some close their eyes, others begin doing repetitive movements such as rocking or playing with a corner of a jacket. Many alter their breathing. Some start to breathe really deeply, as though they were falling asleep. Others make their breathing very shallow.

By far the richest variety shows up in what people do with their minds. Many people simply let their thoughts carry them away. Others pick a particularly attractive fantasy and keep it going. Others remember a time they had that they wish they could relive and do their best to feel that they are back in it. Others choose unfinished business and go over incidents in which they felt wronged. Some get great argumentative cases built. Some make shopping lists or remember song lyrics. There is tremendous variety in what people think about. On the other hand, some people are very good at making their minds blank or foggy. They just space out and don't really know where they've gone.

Another thing that often happens is that many people find that trying to become mindless on purpose makes them really mindful! They have a hard time losing track of the present moment since they know they're trying to do it. Oddly enough, when we practice mindlessness we tend to struggle less. We just give in to whatever distraction comes along. For some of us practicing mindlessness on purpose reveals to us how tightly we hold our minds when we practice mindfulness.

Generating Mindlessness

In the contemplative approach to helping others, we are especially interested in being present with them. We're trying to be mindful when we are with others. The more we know about both mindfulness and mindlessness, the more we can recognize what we're doing and when we're in fact not present. It is also useful for us to know about how mindlessness is cultivated since the people we aspire to help will have such practices too. In contemplative psychotherapy we understand that many people come to therapy because their mindlessness practices are either no longer working well or they are tired of not being more present. That is, either they are feeling more pain or they are feeling inspired to step farther into the world.

I collect mindlessness practices. I am fascinated by the degree of creativity that they often reflect. My students, friends, and clients have been very generous in sharing a great many such practices with me. It turns out that we can turn almost anything into a mindlessness practice! Even sitting practice can be perverted in this way. Later in the book we will look at how to tap this rich resource in our helping activity, but first, let us understand how mindlessness is developed and maintained.

Mindlessness is always dependent on the degree to which we can disconnect body and mind. We could see this as desynchronization of body and mind. For example, the body is in a room with a friend who is telling us about her hard day, and the mind is busy thinking about what would happen if she told off her awful boyfriend. The mind isn't here with the friend. The mind is somewhere else. Or the mind is looking into the refrigerator deciding what to cook for dinner. We all know what it is like to suddenly wake up when we're driving and not know if we've missed our turn or not.

One of my professors would take a piece of chalk and write a few words on the board at the beginning of the class. For the next two hours he would never write anything on the board again. His mindlessness practice was chalk rolling. The mindlessness of it was obvious because he got the chalk all over his hand, all over his clothing, and all over his hair—every week. I don't think he was aware of it.

Mindlessness practices split our attention so that we're not completely present. There are degrees of it. The professor who rolled chalk was fairly present. The body was here rolling the chalk, but the mind and the chalk were not together. He was giving his lecture and a very flat lecture it was. It seemed to be one he had given many times before. There was little vitality in him or connection with the students in the class.

At the other extreme are practices that totally desynchronize body and mind. We see this in the extreme pathology of psychosis when people become lost in a private world and are not able to connect very much at all with others. While most of us do not disconnect this much, we all have practices that take us in that direction. Sometimes just letting our posture collapse makes us dull and spacy.

Many mindless body practices involve playing with or manipulating something. Lots of people play with the keys or coins in their pockets.

Cigarette and pipe smoking contain many opportunities to fiddle around with matches, lighters, and so on. When I teach about this, all I usually have to do is look around the room for examples. Often I can spot quite a number: gum chewing, pen playing, earring manipulating, hair twirling.

I am well known among my students for paper clip twiddling. As soon as I give the lecture on the development of mindlessness, they say, "Oh, look what you do with paper clips!" I still find myself doing it. I'll put one down and at some point later, it's back in my hand. And I don't remember picking it up.

In general, addictions can also be understood as mindlessness practices. Reaching for a cigarette or a drink as a way of being less present is common. Going shopping when we don't really need to buy anything can be a mindlessness practice. We fall into such patterns because they're familiar and they have a quality of sameness to them—always stopping for coffee at the same café, washing the car every week whether it needs it or not, going jogging even if we're ill.

Having a cigarette or a drink is not automatically the cultivation of mindlessness. Jogging or washing the car might not be problems. None of the things I've already mentioned is by nature a mindlessness practice. What makes something a mindlessness practice is the state of mind that it evokes, a fuzzy-edged, not-fully-present, dulled-out state of mind.

We can elicit this state of mind by manipulating our speech also. We might find ourselves sometimes singing a song or repeating a catchy phrase. We might surprise ourselves by discovering that we've been talking out loud without realizing it.

I have a friend who discovered that she had a chattering practice. She realized that when she was nervous at work, especially talking to her boss, she would fall into speaking quickly and without paying much attention to what she was saying. The effect of this was to make her feel somewhat removed from what was happening. It also tended to make her boss go away. Since she was uneasy around him, it brought some temporary relief. Of course, in the long run it was not a great idea to impress on her boss the idea that she was a dithering dodo.

In the movie *Rainman,* the main character has a lovely mindless speech practice. When Raymond gets frightened, especially in unfamiliar situations, he begins reciting the Abbott and Costello comic dialogue of "Who's on first?", accompanying it with the body practice of rocking back and forth. He is then so unavailable that he does not respond to others trying to communicate with him.

There are mindlessness practices that happen entirely within the space of the mind: obsessing, fantasizing, hallucinating. The beauty of these practices is that we can indulge in them and perhaps no one else can tell. I worked with a woman once who had a very elaborate fantasizing practice. She could get so lost in thought that she would forget to take care of simple things like eating and sleeping. Many people these days get so involved in working on their computers that they lose track of needing to eat or go to the bathroom. Often it is these needs that bring them back to the present moment.

Some practices require a certain amount of preparation and planning. My particular favorite is reading mysteries, and so I usually make sure I have a good supply. I even reread mysteries—I already know how they turn out, and yet I read them again.

We have a lot of metaphors for the state of mind produced by mindlessness practices. Most of them contain the idea of mind and body being in different locations: lost in thought, out to lunch, off the wall, off our rocker. These are metaphors for not being present. Other metaphors point to the sense of something missing: playing with half a deck, not firing on all our cylinders, a couple of sandwiches shy of a picnic. A friend of mine recently described her cat in this way, "Her little elevator doesn't go all the way to the top floor." Or we say, "The light's on, but nobody's home."

When are we likely to turn to our mindlessness practices? In general, we begin to separate body and mind when we feel what we called "shock" in the last chapter. When we reach conviction, we have successfully closed off part of our experience. Then we use mindlessness practices to maintain our loss of connection.

We are most apt to indulge in mindlessness when we feel surprised or threatened. Like children turning to security blankets, we turn to these habitual patterns when we feel anxious or uneasy. We are seeking the familiar and soothing. To some extent, this is what we find. We often find that we have taken the edge off things.

On the other hand, mindlessness practices are never totally successful. Other people, situations, and our own brilliant sanity have a way of creeping in. It is good that they do, because mindlessness comes with a price: we miss a lot of our life. We lose our sense of aliveness and responsiveness.

Recognizing Mindlessness

When we are interrupted in our mindlessness practices, typically what arises is irritation, anger, or resistance. Rather than saying, "Thank you so much for waking me up," we're likely to snap rudely at the person who "disrupts our concentration." The first and most obvious hallmark of a mindlessness practice is that we become irritated or aggressive when it is interrupted or interfered with.

Regarding oneself as a helpful person can become a mindlessness practice. We might persistently keep offering our help even when it is rejected. If this rejection irritates us, it's a tip-off that we've become mindless and are offering "help" without being fully present to the situation.

An interesting mindless practice is hypochondriasis—being fascinated and obsessed with one's bodily symptoms. It would seem all of that obsession with what's going on with the body could be mindful. But it somehow isn't. We might find ourselves going over and over some symptom and our fears about what it might mean. "This pimple is probably skin cancer and the cancer is going to spread and then I'm going to die." If someone starts offering us suggestions, what happens? We become cranky or defensive. "Oh, I know all about that already." Or, "That would never work for me."

It's not, "Oh, thank you so much. I really wanted to get rid of this. I'm so relieved." Becoming irritated when we are prevented from running our habitual pattern is a definite sign that we're not feeling open.

A second hallmark of mindlessness practice is loss of curiosity. We are not interested in what the present moment is bringing. We would rather stay with our little world. Rather than give up our video game, we might miss dinner. When we wake up in the middle of the night and we have obsessive thoughts running, how big is the world? Isn't it little? Even though the thoughts might be far ranging, there's a claustrophobic and thick quality to them. They're not very productive.

A third hallmark that is often present is an increasing speed of mind. Sometimes we have become so busy that everything in our mind is a blur. Thoughts are overlapping one over the other, and we cannot really see them as separate from each other. There is very little possibility of seeing any gap in which sanity can be recognized.

Most important, when we are involved in the cultivation of

mindlessness, we tend to lose track of our compassion. Sometimes this is just what we are trying to do. We're afraid that it is too painful to see someone else's distress, so we try to tone things down and not feel so much. When the horror of the war in Bosnia is on the evening news, we may be tempted to turn to a nice soothing, mindless sitcom.

My suggestion is that we become curious about our mindlessness practices. It is very important to bring to them a quality of gentleness and maitri. We may be tempted to try to simply cut them out. The temptation is to declare war on our mindlessness. But this is not a good idea. First, it probably won't work. Second, it would be perpetrating the same aggression that underlies them to begin with. When we invest ourselves in mindlessness we are rejecting our real and present experience. That is the activity of aggression.

Instead, we can start by getting to know our practices really well. We can become experts on how we do what we do. For example, if Ronnie is a hair twirler, he can get interested in how he knows which section of hair to twirl. How does he know how tightly to twist it? What happens to his relationships with other people when he is doing it? When does he do it? How does he feel when he realizes that he is sitting with his hand in his hair? What is his mind like when he is in the middle of the practice?

By bringing curiosity and maitri to our mindlessness practices we have already transformed them into opportunities to be mindful and gentle. In chapter 19 we will return again to mindlessness practices, seeing how we can make use of them in helping others.

11
Gateways between Confusion and Brilliant Sanity

NOW THAT WE HAVE a sense of how we lose touch with our brilliant sanity over and over again and how we maintain that loss through mindlessness practices, it is time to look into how we can make the journey back to ourselves.

It might seem that we need to acquire some new raw materials, tools, and skills for the undertaking, but that's not so. We already have what we need. The very same things that we do to become confused can be turned around and used to help us reconnect to our brilliant sanity. The steps are the same: shock, uncertainty, and conviction. The only difference is in how we deal with these experiences. If we look closely, we can see the seeds of wakefulness within each of these three stages.

Shock as Freshness

As we have seen, shock is our experience when we meet with the unexpected. To use different words, shock is our experience when we discover freshness or novelty. When we develop confusion, we react to freshness by rejecting it. Rather than opening the window and letting clean air into our stuffy house, we would rather keep the familiar stale atmosphere.

Yet many of our most joyful moments come when we least expect them. Situations that begin badly can somehow turn out to be the very best. For example, a teenage girl told me the story of a dance she had attended. As she was getting ready, she tore her new dress. She had to wear an old one. Then she lost her locket, the one given to her by her grandmother. She was already late because of the torn dress, and in her frantic search for the locket, she knocked over a whole bottle of perfume on herself. Now she reeked of perfume. She felt more and more clumsy and unattractive. She almost gave up. Then, she caught sight of herself in a mirror. There were tears running down her face, she was in her old dress, and she noticed that she was in worse shape now than when she had begun the process of "getting pretty to go out." Suddenly, the whole thing struck her as funny. She began to laugh and with the laughter came relaxation. She went to the dance and had a great time.

As we have said, shock is often our response to the three marks of existence: impermanence, egolessness, and suffering. Yet if we are willing to relate with them directly instead of pulling back from them, they are the sun of brilliant sanity shining through the clouds of our mistaken conviction in who we think we are. Indeed, it is only because we are trying to hang on to the untrue story—that we can always be happy, that things won't change without our say-so, and that we are who we believe ourselves to be—that we find freshness to be a shock at all.

If we are not committed to maintaining some kind of status quo, then we are open to the ever-changing flow of our lives. In that stream of events, freshness is natural. When we are not struggling to get things to be other than how they really are, we can see that there is nothing permanent in our experience. Buddhists sometimes describe us as having "mindstreams" rather than minds. This is what we might find in our meditation practice. Instead of finding anything fixed and unchanging, we find a constantly shifting river in which emotions and thoughts and sensations come and go.

Usually we try to freeze our experience and regard it as solid. But just when we think we've gotten things safely fixed, we find ourselves in the middle of a January thaw. Our petty preferences melt in the sudden warmth. We realize, once again, that both we and our worlds are filled with impermanence and egolessness.

I know a woman who trained in college to be a high school teacher. She took a job teaching English and enjoyed it very much for about two years. Then she discovered that she was much more interested in her students' personal issues than she was in teaching grammar and literature. Her first response to this was to push it away. Why would she waste all her training? How could she ever deal with the training she would have to undertake to follow her interests? Besides, everyone knew that she loved teaching. What would people think of her? How fickle and unreliable!

This young teacher's shifting interests came first as a shock, not as welcome freshness. She continued to teach. But she found it was taking more and more effort to do her job. Her heart wasn't in it. Finally, she admitted to herself that she wanted to make a change, and with that came a letting go. She let go of her self-definition as a happy high school teacher and began to explore what she needed to do to become a counselor. She went back to school, which required still more letting go. She found that each step brought up freshness and shock. Now she was a student again. Her income dropped dramatically. She met new people. She had assignments and received grades on them. This was quite a change from being the teacher!

If we can recognize unexpected experiences as freshness, as invitations to nowness, we can transform them into opportunities to wake up instead of making them the first step in developing confusion. We can bring curiosity and openness to them.

We can begin by noticing what our experience is on the spot. What do we feel in our bodies? What emotions are arising and dissolving? What are our thoughts?

Instead of judging what arises as an interference with how we think things should go, we can let ourselves open up just a bit more, let ourselves be present. Like the teenage girl who abruptly saw the humor in her situation, we can open up the narrow view we've become stuck in and take a bigger perspective.

Uncertainty as Open Mind

In the development of confusion, shock is followed by uncertainty. In reconnecting with our basic sanity, shock, or freshness, is also followed by uncertainty. The difference lies in how we work with our uncertainty: we go toward our experience instead of pulling away. Rather than letting uncertainty be an occasion for letting mind and body disconnect, we can use it to bring mind and body together. We can start to know intimately what uncertainty feels like. When it arises it can then remind us to ground ourselves by coming more completely and mindfully into our bodies and environment. In that way, uncertainty itself helps us become present.

Uncertainty is just another word for openness or spaciousness. We are uncertain because we don't know yet. For many of us this feeling is unfamiliar and we tend to judge it negatively. But, as we have discussed before, it is only when we are willing to be present and open that we can really understand what is happening.

The Korean Zen teacher Seung Sahn tells his students, "Only don't know!" Suzuki Roshi, a Japanese master, used to tell his students that the beginner's mind is an empty mind, a ready mind. Even the feeling of stupidity—of not knowing—can be understood to be the sanity of openness. When our minds are filled with certainty—with opinions, judgments, and fixed roles—we are not really present. We cannot see what is right in front of us.

It is sad that so many of us have learned that we should pretend to know when we do not, that it is somehow not all right not to know. In school most of us were rewarded for having the right answer, not for saying, "I'm still thinking about that, I don't know what I think about that yet." How much trouble we could save ourselves (and everybody else) if we could wait until we know more before we act!

It requires courage to remain open and uncertain. If we can stay with our uncertainty and the fear that might arise with it, we can learn to relax with our open minds. Many of us have learned that the quivery feeling that comes with not knowing is "bad." It is often labeled anxiety or fear.

When we are uncertain because we are in the process of letting go of a false sense of who we are, we might feel as if we don't know who we are or what we believe. Sometimes people are afraid that this shaky and tender feeling is a sign that they are becoming crazy. I often hear clients say something like, "I don't know who I am anymore. I must be losing my mind." Ironically, if we can be with this experience and not push it out of awareness, it is the path to reclaiming our sanity and wisdom.

Another thing that we can regard as the emergence of brilliant sanity, but which we sometimes view as a problem, is the experience of doubt. When we have been sure of who we are or what we believe, it can feel shocking to notice doubts. Our tendency is to talk ourselves out of them or to berate ourselves for having them. We accuse ourselves of disloyalty or shallowness.

When we find ourselves questioning, for example, what we have always believed to be the true story of our childhood, we may feel quite uneasy. I remember a colleague of mine describing the bewilderment she felt in trying to put together her warm feelings toward her father with memories of having been beaten with a belt for unexplained misdeeds. For years she had had the knowledge of what happened but had prevented herself from feeling the hurt and anger that arose with it. When she would talk of the memory of being struck, her voice had a very matter-of-fact quality. In order to keep her story simple and convincing, she had pushed aside the feelings connected to her experience. This, in turn, had also shown up as her having difficulty in dealing with ordinary conflicts in her present life. At the first hint of anger or fear, she would squash her feelings down and start to disconnect from herself. Rather than deal with conflicts creatively, she would end up feeling trapped and helpless. She tried her best to avoid situations that might cause conflicts. (This tends to make one's world extremely narrow!)

As she began to experiment with letting her feelings simply be what they were, she found that she could remain present. Her skills in dealing with disagreement and discord began to improve. With respect to her father, she found she was able to love this man who was often so kind to her, and also feel her bewilderment and hurt at his inexplicable temper. She could think of him without having to reach a conclusion or judgment. In order to do this, she had to give up having a tidy story about him. She lost her description of him and of herself without having a good new story to replace the old one.

Conviction in Brilliant Sanity

To review our steps this far: when we bring openness, curiosity, and gentleness to our experience, shock can be recognized as freshness and uncertainty can be appreciated as open mind. We might think that conviction needs to turn into something less certain. But, oddly enough, when we are willing to ride our uncertainty, what often follows is a new kind of certainty. When we are fully present, with minds and bodies connected and grounded, we may discover a conviction of our brilliant sanity. We may realize that we are workable just as we are. In other words, we realize that we are good and tenderhearted people who long to alleviate unnecessary suffering.

When we are present with mind and body together, we can know how we feel. We no longer have to substitute concepts for direct experience. If we feel afraid, we are not confused about it. If we feel confusion, we know that too. We can practice touch and go with our experience whatever it is.

When we are willing to be uncertain, we do not have to maintain any fictional story of who we are. All of our ego stories become irrelevant. There is nothing that has to be given up; instead we can simply see the senselessness of trying to be what we are not. From the contemplative view, ego never existed, so there is nothing that we really have that we need to get rid of.

Completely seeing through ego is, of course, a gradual process, but we find that we have more and more glimpses of freedom from its limitations. Many times the path of reconnecting with ourselves seems to work backward. Often we begin with confused conviction and start to experience just a whisper of doubt. Or a long-held belief that we cannot feel all our feelings comes into question when we allow a painful feeling to arise for a moment without pushing it away.

There is no correct order to experiencing the three stages of reconnecting with sanity. If we use shock, uncertainty, and conviction as opportunities in which to take the time to bring mind and body together, they become gateways that lead us back home to sanity. Whenever we have an inkling that we are caught in any one of them, heading toward confusion, we can remind ourselves that we can bring mindfulness and maitri to this very moment and stop our habitual momentum toward losing touch with ourselves. In this way the very things that tend to be regarded as problems can become valuable allies: situations we fear, changes in plans, disappointments, even insults.

They can lead us to let go of false convictions by rousing our doubts and uncertainties and inviting a fresh look.

As we become more at home with the vividness of all the aspects of our experience—both on and off the cushion—we develop confidence in our basic healthiness and the courage to ride whatever comes up. This lets us open still further.

The less energy that goes into the futile activity of propping up a nonexistent ego, the more fully alive we can become. The less we have to protect, the more we are able to see clearly what is happening and take effective and appropriate action. The less we shield our hearts, the more compassion shines forth to warm us all.

Part Four

Expressing Genuine Relationship

12 Hospitality

IN THIS PART we will discuss going beyond the cultivation of maitri for ourselves and turn our attention to extending ourselves, offering the hospitality that invites others to contact their own basic goodness and brilliant sanity. We will take a look at the basic skills of interaction: exchange, listening, inquiring, and working with feedback.

Up to now we have been focusing on how we work with ourselves. Now, it is time to invite others into our world and for us to go visiting in theirs. As we have said, the most important thing we have to offer to others is simply our ability to be present, open, and welcoming, like hosts who greet their guests with graciousness and warmth.

When I think of really good hosts, I think of a very generous woman I knew years ago. Whenever she invited me over to her home, she always gave me the feeling that I was a special guest she was delighted to see. She would take my coat, offer me a comfortable seat, and give me something delicious to drink. Though she was many years older than I was, she would ask me questions about myself and listen with great attentiveness to what I told her. She told wonderfully entertaining stories about her own youthful adventures and the people she had known. I once attended a birthday party for this lovely lady at which one of the guests raised an interesting toast to her. "To Margaret, who has the uncanny talent of making everyone feel that they are fascinating and special!"

Margaret was expert at creating a sense of welcome and appreciation. She showed her appreciation of her guests in a great many ways—from her attention to physical details like the arrangement of the chairs in her sitting room, which fostered intimate conversations, and the care she took in providing one's favorite cake, to the wholly focused quality of her listening. Nothing was too trivial for Margaret's interest. She was a truly gracious host.

Pseudohospitality

Before we look at how to extend genuine hospitality, let's look at some things that sometimes pass for hospitality but are not. We could call them styles of pseudohospitality.

The first one is a false or fixed sense of separation between us and whoever we're trying to help. At its worst, it takes the form of arrogance in which helpers regard themselves as better than or fundamentally different from those who need help. We might have the feeling that we are saner, more together, better than, or higher than the other person, who is seen as distant and lowly. This perspective is somewhat engrained in our society. For example, R. D. Laing described how in his psychiatric training he was warned that people with schizophrenia were actually different from normal people and that it was therefore impossible to communicate with them.

A contemplative approach based on the view of brilliant sanity understands that we are all basically sane and good. No one's basic sanity is better than anyone else's. We are fundamentally equal. We may be more or less in touch with that sanity, but there is no foundation to support a belief that helpers are better than the people they help.

Actually, we are all helpers as well as people who need help. I got a call one day from a good friend of mine. She was crying, upset that her fiancé had just broken off their engagement. I invited her to come over. We had just settled ourselves at the kitchen table with some tea when I suddenly noticed that my elderly dog was missing. In a split second our roles changed. Instead of me being the comforter and her being the comforted, in an instant she became the helper as I spiraled quickly into fear. We ran out into the yard. Sure enough, the gate had been left open and Molly was gone. My friend took charge. "You look down the street and I'll knock on doors going this way." Two hours later, she located the dog. A neighbor had taken her in since she'd seemed disoriented and ill. Gratefully, we took her home. In the car, driving back, we shifted again. My friend's tears began even as mine subsided. We are all candidates for both offering and receiving help.

Another thing that is not hospitality is having an attitude that we should not have any boundaries. Sometimes people think hospitality means that we just let people come in and walk all over us. Whatever they want, that's just fine. That's not hospitality. That approach requires a tremendous amount of ignorance, the opposite of wakeful hospitality.

This kind of ignorant pseudohospitality reminds me of some hippie-style homes from the sixties and seventies, places where one could come and go and no one cared. If you wanted to crash that was fine. If you brought food, that was good; if not, that was fine too. Clearly there were some tremendously generous impulses at work. On the other hand, these places were often dirty and confusing. There was often an absence of dignity and upliftedness. While there was often warmth, there was rarely clarity or mindfulness.

A good host lets us know where the food is, where to put our coats, and so on. A sloppy host does not tell us. Most people are more comfortable knowing where to find things and feeling that their presence is acknowledged and welcomed.

As helpers, we can let others know where our boundaries lie. If we can be available only some of the time, we can let others know that. If we are quite happy to receive phone calls in the middle of the night we can say that, too. This is often quite an issue for helpers. We can get caught up feeling that we are being selfish and inhospitable if we set any limits on what we can offer. It is important to work with these feelings and see what we can about what story lines they reflect.

For example, if I don't want to say no to someone maybe it's really because I believe that I don't deserve to be treated decently. In meditation, and in some supervision techniques we will look at later, I might uncover this belief, which allows me to question it. Is this really true? Do I really deserve to be treated so unkindly? Is it really helpful to others to let them treat me this way?

Another important boundary has to do with taking on problems we don't feel qualified to handle. This is true whether one is a professional or a nonprofessional helper. Professionals often refer clients to other professionals who specialize in a particular area. At the end of the book is an appendix about when to call in additional assistance.

Another time when we might not be qualified to help is when we are the cause of the problem. If we just fired an employee, we might feel terrible and want to help, but we are probably not the best choice. We can't be the truck that causes a crash and also be the ambulance. Sometimes it is much kinder to find someone else to help or to encourage people to seek out other support elsewhere themselves.

A third kind of pseudohospitality is overwhelming others with our generosity. We make a million suggestions. We show an enormous amount of concern. We worry about them. We call them up. We send them books and articles. We're available to them at all times, whether they want us to be or not, whether they need us to be or not. We leave no gaps whatsoever. We fill up every possible minute by talking about something or presenting an idea and going on and on and on like that. It gives others the message that they have nothing whatsoever to offer—that they are without resources of their own. This "mad Jewish mother" approach undermines our true desire to help. Instead of really helping, we convince the other person that they are helpless without us. Whom is this serving?

A fourth kind of pseudohospitality is the me-too approach. Somebody says something, and we say, "Yes, yes, I understand completely. I have exactly the same thing going on. I know just what you mean." It prevents a recognition of the unique experience that the other person is having. I think it comes from our discomfort with being alone in our own experience. We are all connected yet we are each alone too.

Sometimes people find this kind of comment comforting. Other times it is extremely irritating. It seems to depend a lot on the intention of the helper. If we say it so we don't feel so alone, it's probably not much help. On the other hand, someone who is afraid that if he starts weeping that he will never stop may be comforted to know that we have felt that way too, but here we are having survived.

The last kind of pseudohospitality, which I have seen in action, is hardly deserving of even that name. This occurs when the "helper" takes advantage of the one who needs assistance. What begins as a comforting shoulder to cry on but turns into a sexual advance is very confusing for the person who is already upset. Often this person feels grateful for the attention and comfort and doesn't know how to say, "I appreciate your help, but go away, that's not what I want right now." We've all heard stories of people preying on the newly bereaved. None of us wants to be such a vulture, but this activity can be quite subtle if we're not clear about our intentions. We might even convince ourselves that we are doing something for the other person's good. Once again, our diligence in working with ourselves is very helpful in showing us what we're up to.

Genuine Hospitality

How can we provide the real quality of hospitality to those we would like to help? Obviously, we can't always bring along fine china, gourmet food, and cozy sofas. Nonetheless, we can bring the heart of hospitality to our relationships with others by bringing what we already have.

A good friend of mine who lives in a small mountain community in the Rockies tells a story that captures the spirit of this kind of hospitality. It seems that an older man who lived down the road from her had died, and my friend had been on hand. As the word traveled through the small town that Jesse had died, many people came by to offer their condolences and to bring casseroles and offers of help to his widow. Then one more person came knocking at the door. My friend opened the door to one of the town's women who was regarded as something of a character. She stood on the stoop holding a grapefruit in each hand. "I wanted to bring something, and this is all that I had," she said.

My friend never tells this story without tears coming to her eyes. It doesn't matter whether we show up with Royal Doulton china or with grapefruits. What matters is that we show up and bring whatever we have to share.

In the Mahayana Buddhist tradition, people who dedicate themselves to working for the benefit of others are called bodhisattvas. The conclusion of the bodhisattva vow that is taken by those who aspire to such selfless service is to invite all beings to become their guests. It is like always holding an open house.

When we have an open house, we open our doors and we

say everyone can come. No one has to bring an invitation, no one has to meet a dress code. We don't go to the door and say, "You can come. You can't come. You've got a dreadful tie, you stay out. You're the wrong age. You're the wrong color. You're the wrong sexual orientation." Open house doesn't do that. Complete hospitality doesn't do that. It is just open. It's more than open, it's actually welcoming. It's appreciative of all the people who show up. The basic attitude is that all beings are fundamentally worthwhile—fundamentally, basically good. We are delighted to see them and we rejoice in their progress in waking up. This kind of attitude comes from a conviction in brilliant sanity. If we have such a heartfelt conviction, then this attitude flows naturally from us. To whatever extent we have it, we will be able to provide hospitality.

Most of us are not as open and generous as bodhisattvas, but we may aspire to that kind of generosity. It is important, of course, that we do what we can actually do and not pretend that we are capable of what we are not. As we mentioned above, ignoring our own limitations and boundaries is not hospitality, it's self-aggression. So, we bring what we have and we do what we can do. And usually, it's quite a bit.

Offering genuine hospitality to those we'd like to help is like inviting guests to our home. The first thing that most of us do to prepare for guests is to make the space inviting, and we begin by cleaning. We get rid of clutter, we put away things that belong somewhere else, we polish the silver, we wash the dishes, we vacuum the floors. We make it clean. We get rid of the mess. As helpers, we could do the same thing with our minds. We could clean things up. We could clarify our intentions, which we've already talked about. We could identify and let go of our preconceptions, our expectations, and anything else that is an obstacle to our being fully present, as sane as we can be, and able to make use of our own resources. It's a kind of housecleaning.

It's as if we are a cup of hot water and the other person is a kind of tea. If we are really willing to be present, then we will begin to taste what kind of tea happens when our hot water comes together with the other person's leaves. If we haven't cleaned up—haven't worked with our own minds—then the tea is going to be pretty strange and we won't know how the other person "tastes."

When we invite people over and want to provide hospitality, we don't simply present them with an empty clean house, we also gather flowers, make wonderful food, pick out lovely music, and offer them something nice to drink. We take the best we have to offer and make it available. I think of this as gathering offerings. Making offerings is a traditional practice of generosity in many traditions. We could take the same attitude in our work with others.

At the most basic level, we simply attend to the physical environment that we create or into which we invite others. We try to make it welcoming and warm. We provide a place for people to sit, and their chairs aren't lower than ours. We make sure it's not too bright or too dark. We pay attention to all of those kinds of details of how we create a welcoming space. Sometimes we have no say about where we'll be, but often we do. Should we meet our friend in a quiet restaurant where we can talk, or perhaps outside for a walk? Probably we won't choose a noisy place with no privacy. Other times we are called upon to be helpful at work and we have very little opportunity to change the environment.

Whether or not we are able to affect the physical environment, we can recognize our own richness. We do this not particularly from the point of view of ego, but from the point of view of not holding back because we feel that we don't have anything to offer. Gathering offerings is also recognizing that we have a lot to offer.

Our resources include all of our confusion. If we have had

any experience being angry or jealous or poverty-stricken or arrogant or speedy, then we have tremendous wealth. It is because of our pain and confusion that we can connect to others' pain and confusion. These things are wealth if we bring awareness and maitri to them. They are not usable wealth, obviously, if we just mindlessly indulge them.

We could also include as a resource rousing a sense of courage, rousing a sense of confidence in ourselves, taking an attitude of fearlessness. The idea is that fearlessness is not getting rid of fear but rather it is touching fear, going beyond fear. If we can experience fear, that's already the beginning of fearlessness. It takes a lot of courage to feel the textures of our fear rather than to try to run from it or ignore it.

Every time I go mountain biking with my friend Sharon, I get to play with this one. I made the mistake of telling her a few years ago that I knew that working with fear was the way to develop confidence. And now I can't get away from it. She rides down into all kinds of strange places, and she yells back at me, "Ride your fear!" It's terrible.

Fearlessness has to do with being willing to feel our fear, it doesn't have to do with becoming superhuman and not having any fear. Not having any fear might be the result of ignorance, because we're ignoring the dangers that are really there. It turns out that when we allow ourselves to feel fear, often what we discover underneath is softness and gentleless. Because we can drop that extra layer of armor, that pretense of being stronger than we are, we find tremendous tenderness.

I once worked with a client at a treatment home who was a very big man, and I'm a relatively little person. He was very angry, and he saw in a moment, in some gap, that I was terrified, because I wasn't pretending that I wasn't. I don't think I could have actually managed to hide my fear—my genuineness was not especially the result of any choice I made. At that particular moment, he turned around and left the room. He told me later how much it had hurt his heart to see that I was frightened. He had experienced a moment of wakefulness and tenderheartedness, of not wanting to hurt anybody. This experience created a connection between us that provided some ground to build on.

The last thing in terms of gathering offerings, and perhaps the most important, is that we provide hospitality by how we work with our minds on the spot. One of the very best things that we can offer to others is our ability to create an atmosphere or environment of maitri and mindfulness. This ability to bring hospitality wherever we go is one of the most fundamental ways we can be genuinely helpful.

Probably everyone has had the experience of coming into a room where the atmosphere is oppressive and heavy. This kind of atmosphere has nothing to do with the quality of the air or the temperature in the room. Maybe we've been at a dinner at a friend's home. We've left the room for a few minutes and when we return something has changed. We left a group of laughing, smiling people, and now there is silence so thick with tension we feel like we're swimming upstream through Jell-O as we reenter. No one has to tell us that something happened while we were gone. Even though we don't know what has happened, suddenly we, too, are feeling tense and uneasy.

This kind of environmental feeling sounds a bit like hocus-pocus, but most of us have had some experience with it. As helpers we want to do our best to bring a different kind of atmosphere to others. How can we do this?

To begin with, we do not want to manipulate situations so that they will fit in with our own ideas about how they should be. That would be therapeutic aggression, which we've already looked at. Instead, we want to bring the same qualities of openness, gentleness, and warmth that we work with in our meditation practice. When we show up with the willingness to share our mindfulness and our maitri, we begin to create an environment of hospitality in which others can tap into their own mindfulness and maitri.

In a later chapter we will look more closely at the idea of exchange, but for now let's just note that when we are with others the emotional tone tends to become shared or exchanged. If I sit down with a client who is feeling frightened, I may start to feel nervous myself. I might even have fantasies of being harmed by this client even though there is no evidence of his being dangerous. I have come to realize that I'm not psychically intuiting unforeseen dangerousness in the client. Rather, I am sharing his terror as he touches some feelings that he first had in an unsafe environment. This is my exchange with the client.

When I notice that I'm feeling physically threatened, I can do several different things. I can get caught up in the story I've created and take various steps to protect myself. I can get so carried away that I begin to convince my client that he is a pretty unacceptable person who shouldn't be allowed out without a keeper. Or I can recognize the feeling of fear and work with it as I do when I practice. That is, I can simply notice what I'm feeling and touch it as completely as I can and then let it go. In other words, I can practice mindfulness and maitri. Interestingly, since exchange goes in both directions, what my client may exchange is just this quality of hospitality. He may begin to relax and be more able to be with his own experience, whatever it is.

When something arises in our minds, in our experience, whether it comes from our own minds, our memories, our thoughts, or whether it arises by way of exchange—however that experience comes up—we join it with awareness. We touch, and we allow it to go. By neither grasping nor rejecting our experience, we practice maitri on the spot ourselves. This helps create an atmosphere of maitri in the relationship. For many people, this may be their first experience of maitri, being with us as we work with our minds right there when we're with them.

Providing genuine hospitality is the first step in extending ourselves to others. It is often the most important and useful thing we can do. Creating an environment of maitri, an atmosphere of openness and warmth, requires no special equipment and, happily, is completely portable.

13
Open House of the Heart

WHEN WE ARE WILLING to be hospitable to others, we are opening the doors to our hearts. We never know what we may be inviting when we let others know that we are available and ready to help. If we are really willing to be genuinely present with others we will find that we get much more than we may have bargained for.

On the positive side, we may discover a great well of joy in ourselves that seems to overflow with compassion. Great satisfaction and pleasure come with feeling helpful. Moments when we are fully engaged with others are often the times we feel that we are most alive and that our lives are meaningful.

On the other hand, being present for others can be tremendously challenging. When we are willing to feel our intimate connectedness with others, as we do when we are truly there for them, we may feel their pain quite directly. Even if we are willing to take that on, it may be difficult to stay open and present in the face of someone else's anguish and confusion.

Working with Exchange

In the contemplative approach to helping we use the word "exchange" to refer to our direct experience of someone else. Since we're not solid, when we meet someone else there is an intermingling of energy. If we sit with a friend who's very sad, we might find ourselves feeling sad. Our sadness is not merely our response to hearing about what is happening for our friend. It is as though we catch their sadness. Because we're permeable, we actually pick up on how other people feel. We can pick up on speediness, sadness, anger, any feeling. It is all pretty nonconceptual. If we've never heard about this idea, we won't generally recognize exchange, but we do know that there are certain people we prefer to be around. They might not be people who are particularly insightful. Quite probably they will be those who actually feel good or relaxing to be around, who create a particular kind of presence or space by how they are.

Exchange is not a technique but a natural process. We all experience moments in which the distinction between self and other gets blurred. Sometimes we think this is a problem. Psychologists might even describe this as the result of having poor boundaries. From the contemplative point of view, however, exchange is not the sign of a problem, it is the sign of our basic connectedness. Exchange seems to happen whether we are willing to have it happen or not. If we know about it, we can recognize it and make use of it in order to be of benefit to others.

How can we work with exchange in a way that is useful to others? The husband of one of my clients once came in to tell me "his side of things," at his request and with her permission. In response to my questions, he recounted his wife's many disturbing habits. "She is very sloppy. She never washes her hands above the wrist. She leaves food all over the kitchen."

As I was listening, I noticed that I was becoming uneasy and agitated. I started to feel I wanted to get out of the room. I felt a bit frightened and as if I were being pressured. My client's husband seemed composed and relaxed, sitting quietly in his chair and speaking in a soft and controlled voice. What was this nervousness? My first reaction was to try to make the feeling go away by breathing deeply and refocusing my attention on him. But the feelings kept coming up. Finally, I let myself go toward them and really contact them. I touched into the quivery feeling in my belly; I recognized the fearful tone of my thoughts; I noticed the sweatiness of my palms. Then I began to wonder if perhaps he was feeling nervous and pressured by me. I had been asking him a series of questions to get at his issues. Now I sat back and let him tell his story as he wanted. Very soon he shifted his focus and began to talk of his own fear. My feeling of uneasiness subsided too.

We work with exchange in the same way we work with anything else that arises for us. We practice touch and go. When I began to feel uneasy, it was important that I let myself really feel it. Touching the trembling quality in my belly and noticing the desire to leave the room are examples of touching. Touching means letting in whatever we are experiencing and noticing our body sensations, our emotions, and our thoughts and images. Going means letting it go again—not trying to figure it out or manipulate it in any way. Going means not hanging on, but, instead, coming back to the next fresh moment as it arises. In this example, I came back to listening and let go of my agenda of asking questions.

It really didn't matter if my uneasiness came from me or from the husband at that point. In either case, I needed to practice touch and go with it. At the same time, because I knew that I had not come into the session feeling uneasy, and because I was not aware of any reason for me to feel it in response to what this man was saying, I could tentatively guess that he might be feeling that way.

It is often helpful to let the other person know what we are experiencing. For example, I could have said, "As I'm listening to you I notice that I'm feeling uneasy and nervous. Is that what it is like for you too?" Then he might have said, "Yes, I feel that whenever I'm with my wife when she is making a mess." Or he might have said, "Yes, I feel pretty uneasy coming here and answering all your pushy questions." Or he might even have said, "No, I don't feel uneasy at all." In any case, the communication might have opened up. It also might not have. There are no sure-fire methods of opening up genuine communication!

Exchange can be a powerful way of recognizing what is going on for someone else. It is not, of course, the only way we know what is happening. After all, people tell us and they show us. If we don't know about exchange, though, we can make some big mistakes. For one, we might become confused about our own feelings. With my client's husband, for example, I might have mistakenly begun to get lost in wondering why I was so uneasy. I could easily have come up with a variety of story lines—none of which would have been accurate or helpful.

Sometimes we feel angry or helpless through exchange. If we do not recognize that the other person might be feeling these very unpleasant feelings, we might respond by avoiding this person. It is not uncommon to attribute all kinds of qualities to the people we have a difficult time with. Someone who is confused and angry, and around whom we begin to feel confused and angry, can easily become the target of blame and rejection. We might even come up with a good story about why we are angry at this person. "He doesn't even try to be responsible! Why should I try to help him?" But if we looked closely, we might see that it is not the person's actions that give us a hard time: it is how we feel when we are with him.

Being willing to help means having all these unpleasant feelings. Because of our longing to be helpful and our natural compassion, we are inspired to be present even though it is often no fun at all. So we practice touch and go.

Exchange goes in both directions at the same time. In the chapter on hospitality we saw that how we work with our own minds can have a profound impact on the atmosphere of a relationship. If we are willing to bring curiosity and friendliness to our experience, then we help create an environment colored by mindfulness and maitri into which others may come. This, too, is the operation of the process of exchange. Even if we are feeling as if we have no idea what we are doing, as long as we are willing to be present with ourselves this willingness can be a very generous gift for those with us. This is, perhaps, what happened for the husband who began to talk about his own pain when I stopped trying to avoid my own.

Exchange and Compassion

Working with exchange softens us. We begin to see what it is like to be in someone else's place and this leads to compassion. Folk wisdom tells us not to judge others until we've walked a mile in their shoes. Along with listening to others and spending time with them in their world, the process of exchange really shows us what their world feels like to them.

Janie was complaining over lunch about her landlord. "He says that unless we get rid of the dog, we'll have to move." As she continued to talk, she was becoming more and more upset. Her friend Carol was feeling antsy and impatient.

"Well, you knew when you moved in that he didn't allow dogs!" she said angrily. This led to more complaining by Janie and even more discomfort for Carol. In addition to feeling uncomfortably impatient, now she was also in the middle of an argument with her friend.

Janie went on to say how she couldn't possibly deal with all this. She began to spin fantasies of dire consequences, all of which were the landlord's fault. Finally Carol exploded, "You don't have to feel like this! You're just making it worse for yourself." "Don't tell me what I have to feel!" Janie retorted.

At this point, Carol felt a jolt of terror. Her heart raced and she felt chilled. "Oh," she thought. "I see." She understood for the first time that Janie was really terrified at the prospect of losing her home and having to move. The reasons why she had to move might be explored fruitfully some other time, but right now the important thing was how deeply scared Janie was.

Perhaps Carol might have noticed this earlier if she hadn't gotten so caught up in wanting to escape her own discomfort. She might have recognized her impatience as a sign of trying to get away from her present experience, but what was important was that when she did notice what she was feeling, she let it in. Touching the fear that suddenly arose let her drop her own agenda about the landlord's regulations and become present for her friend who was feeling so overwhelmed.

In this instance, exchanging with Janie's terror let Carol really see what Janie was dealing with. This let Carol become more available and begin to speak to Janie's fear. "You're really scared, aren't you?"

Letting herself feel what Janie might be going through also let Carol's heart soften. She could imagine what it must be like for Janie: a single mother with two kids, a job she didn't like very much, a small apartment with no room for her beloved dog. Now Janie was having to face the long search for another apartment that would let her kids stay in the same school district, the prospect of finding the money for a deposit, finding a landlord who would allow the dog, packing up, and moving. She was really afraid she would not be able to do it. She might end up on the street with no place to go. This was Janie's world; it was pretty painful to contemplate.

Carol's understanding that Janie was building up her own fear with scary story lines and that she was responsible for her present position because she'd ignored the landlord's requirements in the first place might be accurate, but right now they were not helpful. The first step was to be present with Janie's pain. Only then could Carol find her way to be helpful.

Compassion is sometimes translated as "feeling with" and

that is what working with exchange lets us do. First, it helps us to see deeply—to see what things look like for the other person. Then, it invites us to really feel deeply—to know what it feels like to *be* the other person.

To be of help we have to touch as much as we can. This means letting go of the story lines—the explanations and reasons—and just feeling whatever is arising. Having touched our experience just as we do in our meditation practice, we can let it go again and see what happens next. In this way we can really feel our connection with others, but we don't necessarily have to be swept away by their emotions. This is how exchange helps us recognize our connection with others and lets our hearts soften and open.

Letting Go of the Exchange

Sometimes people are afraid that they will get "stuck" in the exchange. That is, if we let ourselves really feel the anger or sadness that arises with someone else, we'll get lost and never come back to ourselves. A contemplative approach is based on the understanding that there is no "self" to come back to, but that there are ways to work with our tendency to make things solid and fixed. In the same way that we tend to hang on to our own emotions and thoughts, we are likely to stick with the ones that arise through exchange.

How can we work with this? We can begin with our sitting practice. Mindfulness-awareness practice is often very helpful in letting what seems solid begin to melt and dissolve. There are two other important techniques that contemplative helpers use. One is the extended practice of tonglen, detailed in the next chapter. Another is the group practice of body-speech-mind that is also described in a later chapter. But there are also ordinary ways of working with our tendency to hold on to what is exchanged.

The easiest way is to come back to our bodies and our sense perceptions. If we recognize how these are changing all the time, we can see that the feelings and thoughts we are grasping are also impermanent and shifting. Coming back to body and sense perceptions grounds us in the present moment.

Another thing we can do is talk to a third person. If we can do this in a way that lets us be present, talking is often very helpful. On the other hand, if we use our conversation to complain about the situation or recreate the very thing we're trying to let go of, it might actually make things worse.

Once I got a phone call from a woman who was quite agitated, complaining about me and about everyone else in her life. After I hung up the phone I went back to my friend who had been visiting. Very soon I was complaining to him about the woman who called and everyone else in my life. Fortunately this friend understood about exchange and he said, "You're sounding just like the woman you're talking about!" Whoops! Caught in the exchange. Simply having it reflected back to me popped me out of it. However, if my friend had gotten into the complaining with me, it would have made my misery increasingly solid. Worse, if he'd started to argue with me, I might have really dug in my heels and became even more convinced that I was right and he was wrong.

Another way to say this is that if talking to someone else can be done mindfully it can be helpful. If it becomes a mindlessness practice in itself, then it will probably make things worse.

It is a good thing that we all have brilliant sanity. No matter how lost we get in our story lines, there are always chinks in their solidity when we can wake up. When we are doing our sitting practice, at some point we suddenly return to the present moment—without planning and without thought. We're just suddenly back, no longer lost in our fantasies and memories. In the same way, our wandering in exchange gets naturally punctured by our wakefulness. The challenge is to recognize the moments when we are back and shift our allegiance to being present. In sitting, we say "thinking." If it's helpful, we can do the same when we work with exchange.

Working with exchange is an amazingly rich resource. The more we work with it, the more we see how connected we truly are with each other. It softens us and tenderizes our hearts.

14
Generating Compassion

HOW CAN WE DEVELOP the compassion to be willing to open our hearts? On the one hand, compassion sounds like a good idea. No one really wants to be unkind. On the other hand, the idea of holding open house all the time seems quite outrageous and impossible. According to a famous story, in a former lifetime the Buddha saw a tigress with her cubs. They had no food and were in danger of dying of starvation. Because of his great compassion the Buddha gave his body to the tigress to feed her young. The first time I heard this story I was horrified. That's what this is all about? I'm expected to throw myself to the tigers and lions? Forget it!

Sometimes we read about parents who sacrifice their own lives to save their children's. We hear of mothers and fathers who do without food or warm clothing so that their children will be warm and fed. We hear of parents in war who stand between their children and gunfire. When I hear such stories I am full of admiration for the courage and love shown by these parents. It seems beyond what I can do, but I can imagine it.

The ideal of the bodhisattva is to regard all beings with the same kind of love and compassion that parents naturally feel for their children. At the same time, there is a strong recognition that to develop so much compassion requires a long and gradual journey. If I were to offer myself to a tigress today it would be ego doing what ego thought was a spiritually advanced action. This kind of ambition is not what we are trying to develop. Such ambition is really just self-aggression. Instead, we are interested in uncovering the natural tenderness of our hearts so that we can be who we are right now. If we can generate one drop of compassion, that is wonderful. If we can uncover more, that's wonderful too. Whatever we can truly discover can be of help to others.

Using Tonglen to Generate Compassion

We have already looked at the tonglen practice as a way to develop maitri. The full tonglen practice is a traditional method of cultivating our compassion. Tonglen lets us begin right where we are and provides us with a gentle and gradual way to nurture the seeds of compassion that exist in us already. We make use of the very things that seem to be obstacles to compassion: our negative feelings and thoughts.

Flashing on Brilliant Sanity. As we have seen, tonglen has a number of steps. The first step is flashing on our brilliant sanity. We can understand this as a reminder about why we are doing tonglen at all. Because we possess brilliant sanity—openness, awareness, and compassion—we have the aspiration to help others. We do tonglen practice so that we can take this longing to be of benefit and start to transform it into compassionate activity so all of us can recognize our brilliant sanity.

Establishing the Texture. The second stage is working with establishing the rhythm of breathing in the hot, heavy, and dense feeling of confusion and pain and breathing out the cool, light, and bright feeling of relief or brilliant sanity. It is like breathing in the hot, humid, heavy quality of the air in mid-July in New York City, and then breathing out the refreshment of jumping into a cool, clear lake in the mountains. We do this until we've established those textures and that alternating rhythm.

Getting Specific. In the third stage we choose a particular situation. In the extended, full practice of tonglen, this specific situation can be in one's own life or in someone else's. Whichever situation we start with, we breathe in all the feelings of pain associated with it, as much as we can. Then we breathe out something that provides help. We imagine that we or the other person actually feels some relief.

Our most valuable riches in this stage are our own experiences of pain and confusion. If we have ever been angry or jealous or anxious or selfish or disgusted or depressed then we have great resources for this practice. We know what it is like to feel pain, and we can know that it is just as painful for others to feel the same way. Our experiences of suffering reveal our common ground with others. So in this third stage, if we think of someone else's situation, we breathe in that person's pain. We take it away from him and feel it as completely as we can ourselves. Then we breathe out to him relief from that pain. Breathing out and letting the pain dissolve on the outbreath for others is like doing mindfulness-awareness practice for them.

Maybe we have a friend who is feeling very sad and frightened because the relationship she is in might not continue. Right now she is in that uncomfortable position of not yet knowing. We can breathe in the feeling of sadness, fear, and uncertainty for her. We can feel it as completely as possible. Then we can breathe out to her a comforting hug or the understanding that nothing is permanent or the feeling of tenderheartedness. We breathe out whatever is genuine for us in that moment.

Expanding Out. The next stage of tonglen, stage four, is to expand beyond this familiar situation and extend our compassion out as far as we can. Not only do we think of the particular situation, we breathe in the pain of all the other people who are feeling just the same. We imagine breathing in uncertainty and fear for many people. Some people like to start gradually, thinking of those in the same room and expanding out to those in the same town and then to the region and then the whole earth or even the universe. For others it is helpful to begin with those whom we feel affection for and then expand out to those we feel neutral toward and then finally to those we actively dislike or have a hard time with.

The point is to expand beyond our own private world and our own personal preferences. In general, tonglen practice lets us go beyond our habitual styles of dividing up the world into us and them. It lets us recognize, again and again, that our pain is the same as others'.

Last summer, soon after my father died, I did a two-week meditation retreat. One day I was practicing tonglen. When I reached the third stage I breathed in the sorrow and sadness I was feeling. I worked with that for a bit, and then I began to expand it out. I tried to breathe in the sadness and sorrow of others who had lost someone they loved. I thought of people I knew—a friend who had lost her husband, another whose sister had died. And then I expanded farther. I thought of mothers in Rwanda who had lost husbands and sons. I thought of children in Bosnia who were losing parents. Because I knew just what such a loss felt like to me, I could easily touch what it might feel like for them. Then, I let it expand out more. I thought of those who had never had someone in their life who was really there for them the way my father had been for me. I thought then of the many people whose parents have let them down through absence or abuse. I breathed in the sorrow and pain and fear that went along with these images. It seemed as if my heart were breaking. Quite naturally I felt tenderhearted appreciation for all that I had received from my dad. I breathed out this appreciation, not only to myself and to him, but also to all of those who had never felt welcomed and appreciated.

Balance

Tonglen means "sending and taking." It is important to have a balance between the breathing out, or sending, aspect and the breathing in, or taking, aspect. We might find that we tend to emphasize one part more than another. We might be reluctant to take in our own or someone else's pain. Sometimes people wonder if this isn't a kind of self-aggressive or masochistic practice. Actually, it is not. When we breathe in we are simply allowing ourselves to soften and be with what is already there for us. We can remember that brilliant sanity is about the unlimited space that is our nature. When we breathe in, we do so into a huge space that can easily accommodate whatever we need it to. When we practice in this way we may discover this accommodating space. Also, we see that our own and others' pain is not really solid.

If we were to do tonglen from the reference point of ego, cramming more and more stuff into a little space, then it would indeed be self-aggressive. However, tonglen is based on understanding that we have no fixed self and that our nature is open and compassionate. Instead of being self-aggressive, tonglen gives us the opportunity to practice being who we really are. Of course, we need to remember always to do what we can do and not try to push ourselves to meet some idea we have about who we should be and what we should be able to do.

As for breathing out, sometimes people feel they have nothing to send. It may take a little practice, but we find that we really do have lots of wealth to share. Maybe it is something simple like a cup of tea that we can imagine sending, or a really good dinner. Often it is helpful to breathe out the pain and let it dissolve into the huge space of brilliant sanity. We send this to others—the dissolution of their pain.

Another thing that people often ask about is how to make the practice feel more real, and not like just a bunch of thoughts. If we begin with our situation just as we find it, we can breathe in whatever discomfort is present. Maybe it is something obvious like my grief. Or perhaps it is something subtle like the feeling that we don't know how to begin. So we begin with that. We breathe in our uncertainty and the feeling of inadequacy or whatever is there for us in that moment. Then we might breathe out a feeling of maitri, the sense that we can be friendly to our experience whatever it is. We can gradually expand that out to everyone else who is uncertain and doesn't know how to be.

Letting the Practice Develop

We let the practice unfold as it does. If we begin with uncertainty and it turns into another feeling—for example, fear—that's fine. We might find that now we are breathing in the feeling of fear that we and others feel about beginning something unfamiliar. Then, we can breathe out whatever feels like its opposite or what feels like a source of relief. Perhaps we breathe out a feeling of confidence that we can be with whatever comes. In any case, we try to stay with what feels right rather than with our ideas. Tonglen trains our heart and so it is not really an intellectual exercise; it is more of a training ground for our emotions. We work with a particular situation, expand it out, and then go on to the next situation.

If at any point in our practice we notice that we have totally spaced out and forgotten that we are even doing tonglen, we can start again. Sometimes we need to start over at the beginning with step one. Other times we can easily pick up with the present situation or one close at hand. Whatever feels appropriate is probably fine. We can even breathe in whatever it is we feel about having spaced out and go from there.

How long should we practice? Generally, ten or fifteen minutes in the context of an hour's sitting practice is a good guideline. Always sit for a while first and be sure to have time to sit afterward too. In group practice settings, we ring a gong to signal the beginning and end of the tonglen practice. As the sound of the gong dies away at the end, we let ourselves just be with the sound as it dissolves. Then gently we return to our mindfulness practice. If you practice on your own and don't have a gong, you can let yourself have a sense of expanding out into space and allowing a few moments of transition before you gradually pull your attention in to the focus of your mindfulness-awareness sitting practice.

We can also bring the tonglen practice into our lives. Many people find that this is actually easier and more real for them than doing the formal tonglen practice on their cushions. The same basic approach applies even though we may not go through all four stages. Instead, when we are faced with a difficult situation, we simply breathe in whatever pain or discomfort we are feeling. Then we breathe out relief or a sense of spaciousness. If we are starting to feel angry at the service manager where we brought our car to be fixed, we can breathe in our anger—feel it completely. Then, we can breathe out a sense that the anger is ventilated, has lots of room and doesn't need to explode into words. When we can do this we find that we have more of an ability to hear and to be present. We are not trying to get rid of the angry feelings. Actually we are trying to be with them even more than we usually do. When we fully touch in this way we often find that we are no longer so caught by our emotions.

Practicing tonglen with others is a good way to work with exchange too. Whatever is arising for us with someone else can be breathed in fully. Then we can breathe out our compassionate feelings or a sense of relief to the other person.

Tonglen is a powerful tool for developing our inherently compassionate nature. As we have seen, the biggest obstacle to our brilliant sanity is our conviction in ego. Tonglen turns ego on its head. Where ego says, "Give me all the good stuff; you take all the bad stuff," tonglen trains us to practice just the opposite. We breathe in what we would most like to run away from and we give away what we value most. Ironically, the more we let go and give up holding on to the nonexistent self of ego, the softer, more relaxed, and joyful we become.

15
Being a Good Listener

"ABOUT TEN YEARS AGO I was traveling through Oregon. I was having a really hard time then. I was agitated and freaked out. I went to see Chagdud Tulku, a Buddhist teacher. He didn't really do very much, but he listened to me and after a while I somehow became calm." This was related to me by a former student.

One of the ways we show people that we are present with them is by how we listen. Being a good listener seems to come naturally for some people, but most of us benefit from learning some basic listening skills. These are the same techniques taught to students training to be counselors and psychotherapists, and they can be useful to all kinds of helpers.

We often find that instead of listening, we are just waiting to speak. We might be busy planning what we are going to say next. We might even interrupt and jump in with our own ideas. The person who is speaking will quickly understand that we're not really paying attention. Sometimes people shut down when this happens. They stop talking about what matters to them. They stop telling us, and often they stop letting themselves know too. We are sending the message that their experience is not interesting or worthy of attention. Children especially take to heart these unspoken messages.

Basic Listening Skills

The first basic listening skill to practice is really paying attention. From our meditation practice we know that our minds tend to jump around. First we're present and then we're not. The same thing happens when we are with others. We might begin by listening carefully; then suddenly we're lost in our own thoughts about something else. When we notice this, we can gently bring ourselves back. If we've been absent so long that we've lost track of what is being said, we can say so. This lets others know that we really do want to know what they're saying.

We can show that we are following, listening, by nodding and looking at the person who is talking. We can interject brief comments like, "I see," or "Umm hmmm." I have been told that in some cultures the expectation is that when one person talks the other people present listen. In those cultures one is not expected to show that one is listening. It is taken for granted. But most of us in the West don't feel heard unless listeners show us, by their body language or their words, that they are really attending.

Along with paying attention, we can work with allowing silence. We don't have to respond immediately. We can take our time and see what our reaction is and formulate what we want to say. This also helps us drop the pressure to come up with a reply before the other person is done speaking. Some people are not comfortable with silence and tend to fill it up right away. We can feel our way with this. For many, allowing there to be some silence provides an opportunity to slow down a bit. That can be quite a relief in itself. So the first skill of listening is learning to come back, to drop our own distractions, and to allow some space into the conversation.

The second skill is paraphrasing. We let the other person know that we are hearing them by letting them know what we have heard. We put what we have heard into our own words rather than simply repeating the same words as though we were parrots. Obviously, we can't say everything we've heard, but we make a statement that shows that we've heard what's been said.

When I work with couples in counseling, we often spend a lot of time practicing just this skill. We call it stop, say, go. After one partner speaks, the other one says, "This is what I heard you say. Is that right?" If the first speaker agrees that the paraphrase is correct, then the other partner speaks. The first speaker then does the same paraphrasing exercise. Obviously, the conversation gets very slowed down, but each person begins to feel heard. After all, most couples come for help when communication has become problematic, so learning to listen is extremely important.

I remember one couple I worked with: I'll call them Gina and Frank. Gina said something like, "I would like to have some time to do some of the things I used to do before we got married. I would like time to paint and take walks alone."

Frank's first paraphrase was, "You don't want to be with me."

"No, I want some time to do some things alone."

He tried again. "You want to be alone. You're tired of me."

Clearly, Frank was hearing more than Gina was saying. With another try, he got much closer. "You haven't been doing the things you used to do before we got together. You'd like to have some time alone to do things like paint and go for walks." Gina agreed that this was what she had meant. Next it was Frank's turn to speak.

"When you talk about wanting to be alone, I get afraid that you want to leave me and end the marriage."

Gina's first attempts at feeding back what she heard from Frank were not any more accurate than his had been.

"You want me to always be right there where you can see me. You don't trust me at all."

You can imagine the kinds of communication that were going on with both partners mind reading the way they were! Neither one felt heard, and both were quite fed up. Beginning to listen—or even trying to listen—was a powerful message of caring for these two people.

As helpers, we don't usually need to slow things down this much, but the skill involved is the same. We simply let the other person know that we have heard the substance of what they have said.

The next skill builds on this one. This one is listening for the feelings. Instead of just feeding back the content of what is said, in this skill we let the person know what feeling we are hearing in the words. The person may have referred to feelings directly or not.

For example, when Janie was complaining about her landlord and the burdens of looking for a new place to live, Carol could have paraphrased by saying, "Sounds like your landlord is causing you a lot of problems and you'll have a lot to do if you move." A response based on listening for the feelings might go deeper: "It sounds like you're pretty angry at your landlord and scared about finding another place to live."

This kind of listening is more active and invites the speaker to look more closely at what they are experiencing on the spot. Notice that when we reply with either a paraphrase or from listening for the feelings, we do not add anything of our own. All we are doing with these skills is helping others become more clear and present with their full experience.

As a listener we can also help others to focus. A skill we might use here is summarizing what we've heard. We've been listening to Glenn. "You've been talking about the problems you've been having with your boss and also about what's going on with your girlfriend. Now you're starting to talk about your plans for next summer. Would it be helpful to focus on one of those or is talking about a number of different things helpful right now?" Once again, we're not adding our own opinion about what Glenn should choose—or even that he should focus only on one thing. By summarizing we show him what we've heard and give him a chance to decide what he wants to do next.

A very simple technique that we teach to counselors in training is to repeat a word or phrase to show that we are listening. For example, let's look one more time at Gina's first statement about wanting time for herself: "I would like to have some time to do some of the things I used to do before we got married. I would like time to paint and take walks alone."

If I were responding by using this repeating skill, I might say, "Alone?" That seems like the most potent word in what she said. Someone else might pick a different word or phrase to repeat. For example, "Used to do?" or "Paint and take walks?" Each of these would invite a somewhat different response from Gina.

With all of these skills it is important to be really interested, not just to go through the motions that show we are interested and listening. I hear many jokes and see cartoons that make fun of therapists who might, for example, be shown listening to a suicidal client and then saying, "Oh, you're depressed and now you're planning to commit suicide."

Whenever we present the simple repeating skill to counseling students we are likely to get teased by them. I might ask, "Are there any questions?" And students will reply, "Questions?" or "Any?" or even "Are there?"

In my own training, I used to worry about when I should say um hmm and when I should be quiet—as though my timing were so crucial! The most important thing is to really be there with the intention to hear what we are being told. We can trust our basic sanity to decide when to speak up and when to be quiet, when to merely listen and when to get more actively involved. First, though, we need to be able to hear.

Hearing includes not just what we're told in words. We also need to pay attention to tone of voice, body language, and all the clues that are part of communication. I once heard a speaker demonstrate the difference between listening only to the words and listening to the whole message. "I love you!" she shouted in an angry voice. "What would you believe?" she asked us, "My tone or my words?" Most of us believe the nonverbal message first and the words only if they match. When parents' nonverbal and verbal messages are in conflict too often, children grow up very confused and, some people say, are likely to become psychologically disturbed.

Dealing with Our Own Reactions

I've said that when we are listening we don't add anything of our own. Strictly speaking that's not really true. Whenever we listen we pick up on some things and don't pick up on others. This will affect what we respond to, which, in turn, may direct the conversation in one direction and not in another. I don't think we are ever completely neutral, but we can do our best to try to stay with the concerns and priorities of the person we are listening to and not to interject our own agendas. Again, the more we know about our own intentions, the less likely we are mindlessly to impose our own needs on others.

Sometimes we need to let other people know if we cannot put aside our own concerns. If I am trying to help a friend who is agonizing about whether to have an abortion or whether to go ahead with an unplanned pregnancy, it is probably important for me to let her know if I have a strong opinion of my own. If I do, I may or may not be able to listen and help her clarify her own mind. If because of my own mindfulness practice I am aware of the solidity of my views, I need to let her know that I might not be the right person to help with this problem right now and why.

On the other hand, if I tell her where I stand and she still wants to talk with me about her dilemma, maybe that's a clue for her about her own preferences. I find that often people choose to discuss things with someone who will reflect back to them what they really want to hear. That's fine. It's their intelligence at work, and we can make the process more visible by commenting on it.

For example, once a new student came to talk to me about a drug problem with which she was working. She had just stopped smoking marijuana for the first time in a number of years. By telling me—the head of her training program—she was making sure that she could not mindlessly go back to her old habits. She was blowing her cover. If I knew her to be indulging her old habit again, I would not be able to ignore it; it would most likely mean that she would be asked to leave the program. We were able to talk about how risky and intelligent it was for her to choose to discuss her situation with me.

I am often impressed by how important just these simple listening skills are. Many times just being heard is comforting in itself. Sometimes all that people need to become more clear about what to do is to have the chance to air their thoughts and contact their feelings. These basic skills can provide the space and support that help people to see for themselves what to do next.

16

That's a Good Question

AS WE HAVE SEEN, one of the most helpful things we can do for others is to support their efforts to clarify their own thoughts and feelings. The main tools we have for this task are being present, listening well, and asking good questions. In this chapter we will examine some basic skills in asking useful questions.

We probably all know what it is like to be asked questions that are not helpful. It can be irritating, confusing, and distracting when our well-intentioned friends and family rally around and bombard us with a thousand questions or suggestions just when we are trying to sort things out for ourselves.

"Well, why did you invest in that company anyway?" "Who is she going out with now? What did you do to drive her away?" "Isn't this exactly the same thing your father used to do?"

These questions tend to take the person away from their experience in the present moment. They may imply a sense of blame. Or they suggest that the answer is already known before the question is asked.

Probably the worst kind of question is like the old joke: "Answer yes or no, did you stop beating your wife?" Of course, if you never beat your wife, you can't answer with either yes or no. This is an example of asking the wrong question altogether.

How can we ask good and useful questions that lead others to become more clear about how they are feeling, what their concerns are, and what actions they want to take? How can we do this in a way that supports both their intelligence and the development of maitri?

There are some basic skills that we can learn and practice. The first steps in asking good questions are what we have already looked at: being present and listening. The more open we are to really hearing how things are for the other person, the less likely we are to impose our own biases on the situation. So the first step, as always, is to show up with an open mind and heart.

We can then ask questions that are based on the present situation. In general, it is rarely useful to get caught up in how things came to be this way. That might be an interesting pursuit some other time, but when people are in pain and need assistance, tracking history is not usually a helpful approach. It tends to take people away from their present experience, and it gives them the message that we are not as interested in helping as we are in trying to satisfy our own curiosity.

Questions that help people focus on the present moment tend to begin with "what" and "how," and not with "why." Let's look first at why questions.

"Why did you do that?" "Why do you want to hurt me like this?" "Why aren't you more like your brother?"

Why questions invite people to explain and defend themselves. Usually this leads to their feeling attacked or blamed. It may not be our intention to attack or blame, yet it is the response most people feel. When they feel this way, they also feel pushed away by us. They tend to pull back and feel more guarded and wary. This may be just the opposite of what we intended when we asked our question.

Another unwanted result of our asking why questions can be that the others receive the message that we think they are stupid or incompetent. "Why did you do that?" is easily heard as, "You nitwit! Why would anybody in their right mind do that?"

Another problem with why questions, but not limited to them, is that they often veil our own agendas. When we ask, "Why?" we may really be saying, "I think . . ." It looks as if we're asking, but we're really telling. For example, "Why did you accept that position?" may sound like "I never would have taken that position." "Begging the question" means to assume we know the answer and then to ask a question that nearly forces the other person to frame the situation as we have done.

"How come you came to dinner tonight dressed so inappropriately?" Notice that the options available to a teenager addressed in this way are pretty limited. He can defend his choice of attire; he can deny its inappropriateness; he can storm out of the room. What he probably hears is, "You've dressed inappropriately for dinner, and I think you are a bad person." Notice too that "how come" is just another way of saying why.

Finally, why questions invite others into the past; they don't help them become more present now. "Why" suggests that we look at what has already happened—that is not necessarily a bad idea for another occasion. But when help is needed, it is only by coming into the present moment that we can discover where we are and what needs to happen next.

We can try to explore for ourselves by noticing how we feel when others ask us questions that begin with why. Notice the difference in how you respond as you imagine someone asking you, "Why do you feel that?" and "What do you feel?"

Instead of asking why, we can ask how or what. "How does that make you feel?" "How does losing your job affect your plans?" "What do you think about that?" "What options are you considering?"

Questions that begin with how or what tend to open things

up. They invite exploration and curiosity. When we feel distressed we are likely to close down. We may feel as if the world is quite small and options are very limited. We may feel trapped and hopeless. It is as if we are walking around in a dense fog. Things suddenly loom up out of the murkiness, but we can't get a sense of how things go together or what else is there, just out of sight. Our emotions may be in a swirl: we don't know how we feel. Or we feel numb. Anything that helps us to open up a bit, that disperses the fog, can be quite valuable.

Questions that begin with how or what can be good ways to help us focus on what is happening right now. Questions that invite us to be more present with our bodily experiences, with our emotions, and with our thoughts can be very useful.

Tracy just heard the lab results of her annual physical. She has a suspicious-looking cyst on one of her ovaries. Like most of us, it is very easy for her to think of the others she knows who have had ovarian cancer. Her own mother died of it. She can fall into remembering the past and quickly turn that into a dire fantasy about her own future. She can become lost in a tumult of thinking and fear about what might happen. Inviting her back to the present moment and to the reality of uncertainty can help her cut the painful buildup of past- and future-centered thinking. It might even let her touch the appreciation she feels for those who are in her life right now.

Another dimension we can pay attention to when we ask questions is whether our questions are open-ended or closed-ended. We'll call these open or closed questions.

Closed questions call for a one-word or very brief answer. They are often questions that ask for yes or no as the answer. These questions can be helpful when someone is feeling very confused. They can be used to help the person focus and become more grounded in body and environment.

"Can you see me sitting here?" "Do you know where you are?" "How many fingers am I holding up?"

Closed questions can also be used to gather factual information. "Was there anybody else in the car with you when you went into the ditch?" "What's your name?"

The drawback to closed questions is that they may keep the focus narrow when it is more helpful to open things up more.

On the other hand, open questions are good for helping us to explore things and to open up our minds. They are a way of inviting others to relax and let go of any fixed views that may be getting in their way.

"What would happen if you didn't go back to school?" "When you see your girlfriend talking to another guy, what do you imagine is going on?" Compare this question to a why question like, "Why do you get so jealous when you see your girlfriend talking to another guy?" The second one seems more blaming and also assumes that jealousy is the person's response.

Open questions invite the person to tap into their creativity and can also suggest that there is more than one way to look at things. Sometimes this provides welcome relief.

A mistake helpers often make is to ask more than one question at a time. "What are you feeling right now? Do you want to stop talking? Is it okay if I ask you about your mother?" Most people will find a series of questions confusing. More often than not, people answer only the last question asked.

One last thing to keep in mind when we begin to ask questions is whether we have been invited to do so. Any time we present ourselves as helpers it is good to be sensitive when we begin to go deeper. Whenever we ask questions, we are going more deeply into the other person's feelings and thoughts. When people are distressed it is harder for them to tell us that they wish we would go away. It is up to us to try to be sensitive to what is wanted and needed.

I have a friend who is also a therapist. Often our conversations are chatty and humorous. Sometimes one of us will want some help. We have developed a kind of password with each other. "Do you want to really talk about this?" one of us will ask the other. This is a way of asking permission before going farther. There are no sure ways to know when we are being a help instead of a nuisance, but when we are in doubt we can check it out by asking what kind of help would be useful.

Soon after I began dating my husband Fred, I received some unwelcome news from a doctor. When Fred heard the news from me by phone, he asked if it would be helpful to me if he came over. He didn't assume that he knew what I needed. I felt respected and cared for by his thoughtfulness.

Here are some other possible questions. "Would it help if I asked you some questions?" "Is it okay to ask you more about that now?" "Would you rather be alone now?" "Do you know what you'd like me to do?"

If we're told that someone would rather be left alone, we should respect that. We can let the person know how to reach us, or we can stay nearby—for example, in another room—if that seems appropriate. This can be a very important message: we are saying that we respect the person; that we will not aggressively intrude; and that we are really listening.

17
Giving and Receiving Feedback

ALL OF US ARE CALLED UPON to give feedback to others. Giving feedback is telling others about our experience of them. It seems like a very simple task, and yet many of us are extremely uncomfortable performing it. Receiving feedback from others—hearing how others experience us—presents a whole different set of difficulties, and many of us shy away from that as well.

As a faculty member of a clinical training program, I am often in the position of giving and receiving feedback. I have seen that being able to make good use of feedback is one of the most important skills for a helper in training to develop. Students (or, for that matter, faculty and directors) who are unable to hear or make use of feedback cut themselves off from a very potent source of learning. We need to hear from others about how we were doing. At the same time, when it comes to giving feedback to someone else, we may be hesitant to be seen as aggressively marching in and dumping our views uninvited. In an approach grounded in the notion of nonaggression, it presents a dilemma. How can we utilize the tremendous resource represented by hearing from others about ourselves and yet not perpetuate the kind of therapeutically aggressive demand for change that feedback so often seems to imply?

All too often giving feedback has as its aim the desire to get the other person to change so that we ourselves can feel more at ease. Rather than having the intention to provide others with a mirror of their behavior, we have a secret agenda to get them to conform to some notion we hold. We may be quite unaware of this intention. Yet when we look closely, we see that it is often present.

In the early 1970s, the heyday of "sensitivity training," feedback was often the banner under which we said some of the unkindest things to each other. Even today, handouts we may receive about how to give and receive feedback often have a subtle message about how best to tell someone something so that our message will bring the result of supporting our own version of ourselves or of others.

On the other end of things, while receiving feedback, all too often we find ourselves defending ourselves, defending ego, rather than letting in what someone else says. Is it any wonder that we so quickly go into a defensive mode if the intent is fundamentally aggressive? Even when the giver of the feedback's intention is unclouded by aggression, we may find it difficult to simply open and hear what is said.

In order to offer useful feedback to another it is best if we can get our own self-interest out of the way. In order to hear feedback, we need to get our stake in maintaining our self-images out of the way. The best way to overcome the confusion represented by ego is through mindfulness-awareness practice. Giving and receiving feedback can become an interpersonal mindfulness practice, providing opportunities for us to work with our minds on the spot. The very things that make feedback such a delicate and often painful enterprise are the same things that make it a potentially rich contemplative practice.

In meditation practice, we sit alone and work with whatever

technique we have been given. Often we practice gently coming back to the breath as a reference point for the present moment. Our minds wander off again and again, and we learn to recognize the difference between being present and being absorbed in thought. We cultivate our inherent ability to be mindful of the details of our experience. In addition, the gentle recognition of what is happening helps us cultivate maitri, the attitude of unconditional friendliness toward our own or another's experience. Mindfulness practices help us develop both the precision of seeing each moment clearly and the nonaggression of letting each experience be what it is.

The following guidelines can transform giving and receiving feedback into a mindfulness practice. The more we are mindful of our own experience moment to moment, the more we are able to recognize when our intention is to protect ourselves and when our intention is to be helpful to others. Often we find that there is a mixture or alternation of the two. The purpose of practice is to help us become more mindful and aware. Bringing this kind of intention to the feedback task brings both a sharpening of precision and a relaxation of aggression.

Guidelines for Giving Feedback

Have the intention to be of benefit. As we have seen, it is important to recognize the difference between intending to help others and intending to help ourselves at their expense.

Generally, it is a good idea to ask permission before offering feedback to someone. A simple, "Would you like to hear how I experienced that?" or "Can I give you some feedback?" will give the other person a chance to say yes or no.

There are a number of ways to improperly offer feedback. Sometimes we might try to use feedback as a way to unload our negativity on to someone else. Obviously, this is not helpful.

For example, Cheryl has had a really rough morning with the kids and she is wondering if she is a capable parent. She feels pretty rotten. When she gets to the daycare center, one of the staff members asks her how she likes the new program that he has designed. She think it's okay, but once she starts telling him what she doesn't like, she finds that she is getting more and more negative. Her comments are way out of proportion to how she really feels about the program. She's dumping all of her anger and frustration on him.

Another way we might misuse feedback is by falling into therapeutic aggression, which we've looked at before. If we do this, we might, for example, tell a friend what we think of her boyfriend with the secret agenda of getting her to get rid of him since we feel so uncomfortable around him ourselves. We're not really interested in looking at our own discomfort. Instead, we are trying to manipulate our friend.

One other less-than-helpful way to give feedback is to offer positive feedback to people with the hope that this will make them like us. Most of us know some vivid metaphors that describes this kind of behavior in which insincere compliments are paid in order to curry favor. Again, this is not a helpful use of feedback.

Be a clean mirror. Be descriptive, not interpretive or judgmental. Giving feedback is like holding up a mirror for someone else. It is good if we can keep our personal opinions and concerns from fogging up the mirror.

A particularly tricky pitfall we can fall into is giving advice under the pretense of giving feedback. If I look into a mirror and see that there is a dirty smudge on my chin, I can clean it up. The mirror doesn't have to tell me what to do.

For example, suppose we say something like "Joe, you seem a lot less attentive to details at work lately. I wonder if it is because you're unhappy with the recent management change.

You really should do something about that attitude. What I suggest is that you sit down every night and meditate. I can't imagine why you are letting yourself go in this way." Here we have loaded advice, speculation, judgment, and possibly our own dissatisfaction with the management change onto what began as a simple description. Joe is quite likely to feel that we are pushing our own agenda.

To avoid this, we can be descriptive rather than becoming judgmental or interpreting what we have seen. In the same situation, we could simply describe what we've seen and say how we have reacted to it. "Joe, the memo you sent me yesterday had some information left out. I've noticed that you seem to be less attentive to details in the last few days. My reaction has been to wonder if you are unhappy with the management change. Is that something you'd like to talk about?"

In this instance, the speaker has been more specific, has identified the interpretation as such, and has invited Joe to respond or not. Joe could very well decline to discuss it, or he might tell us that something else is making him preoccupied, or he might want to discuss his fears of losing his job, caused by the change in management. In any case, he will now have more information about how others are seeing him, which is the purpose of giving feedback. He can decide for himself how to deal with the smudge on his chin. If he wants advice, he can let us know himself.

Present a balanced view. We can present a more balanced view by paying attention to giving both positive and negative feedback. A roommate might say, "I really appreciate the hard work you have put into fixing up the house. You've really made it more cozy and welcoming. On the other hand, I have noticed lately that when I speak to you, you don't seem to be paying attention. Last Friday we were in the middle of a conversation, and you got up and made a phone call. I ended up with the impression that you do not value what I have to say and I notice that I've stopped talking to you about the things I really care about."

Put yourself in the other person's place. We can consider the readiness of the other person to make use of what we have to say. It is important to pick a time and place for offering feedback that shows respect.

When I was in the ninth grade I had a teacher comment as she returned a paper to me in class, "Karen still believes that 'cheese' is spelled with a 'z'." I was so embarrassed in front of the other students that I've never forgotten either her comments or how to spell cheese. On the other hand I became shy and frightened in her class.

Be specific rather than general. It is more useful to describe specific behavior, not our general impressions of the person. We can refer to specific instances whenever possible instead of getting sidetracked into unrelated matters.

For example, we have been asked to comment on how well a colleague did a clinical presentation. We get caught up in describing how it reminds us of a client we once worked with and we wonder if our colleague feels he is an empathic person or not. If we were more mindful of our own experiences in the moment we might notice an impulse to draw attention to ourselves. The suggestion here is not to follow this impulse.

Own your own experience. When we describe our reactions to another person's behavior, we can acknowledge it as our own. Not blaming is very important in giving feedback. We should share our reactions as information, not as pressure to make the other person change. One way to do this is to begin with "I" instead of with "you." In that way we stick to our own experience rather than guessing what the other person feels.

I might tell someone that when she was late to the last three meetings, I felt angry and did not really want to welcome her into the discussion. I could offer this because I believe it would be useful information to her, not to unload my anger.

Be direct and fearless. We may feel uncomfortable saying something unpleasant to someone. It helps to remember that our intention is to be helpful. Keeping information from someone may be more harmful than offering it.

In an agency where I used to work, everyone was avoiding a certain woman because she had a terrible smell. She smoked cigarettes and seemed to wear the same clothing every day. We avoided telling her, and we did our best to stay away from her as much because of our discomfort at not telling her the truth as because of her smell. She began to believe that no one liked her or appreciated her work. Rather than shying away from the embarrassment or fear that might have arisen in telling her, we could have allowed ourselves to be present with all these feelings, thus opening the way to speaking with her. When I look back on that situation, I wish I'd had the courage to tell her then. Unfortunately, she left the agency without knowing why she had been so isolated.

Another way we can be more clear and direct is to minimize our use of qualifying words. Sometimes people use a great many unnecessary adjectives and adverbs in their attempts to soften what they are trying to say. The result can be so vague that the listener has no idea what's been said.

"Well, you know, I kind of think that what you said yesterday was sort of a little bit not so great if you know what I mean." This is an extreme example, but I've actually heard things that were nearly, you know, kind of equally ridiculous.

Say your piece and let it go. It is easy to become attached to what others do with our feedback. Instead, we could let it be an offering, an expression of generosity. If feedback is valuable to others, they will make use of it in their own ways. It is not important that we get acknowledgment or see the results of how the feedback is used. Sometimes it takes a long time to incorporate feedback; at other times our feedback is simply not relevant to the person who hears it. Our task is to offer it and then to let go of any expectations we have about how it will be used.

This does not mean that there are no consequences. A boss, for example, giving feedback to an employee can be clear that unless the issue is addressed as the boss wants, the employee will be out of a job. Then it is up to the employee to make his or her own decision. The point is to be clear, not to get people to make the decisions we want them to make.

Guidelines for Hearing Feedback

We probably all have been the recipients of feedback—solicited or not—ranging from the kindly given to the aggressively and unskillfully given. In general, it is a challenging task to listen to what is offered to us as feedback. Here are some guidelines that can help us use these opportunities to develop our mindfulness and to improve our skills as helpers.

Have an open mind. We can put our efforts into simply hearing what is being said. We do not have to assume that we already know what the other person means. If we need to, we can ask for clarification.

If a coach tells a basketball player that he is a poor team member, he can ask the coach what that means. (Not, "What do you mean, you moron!" but "What do you mean? I'm not sure I understand what you think the problem is.") Then the coach can get more specific. Maybe he means the player is caught up in his own concerns and is not available when his teammates want to pass to him, or that he tends to take the ball and run with it, ignoring his teammates. Those are very different messages.

Be curious about your state of mind. We can notice what arises in our minds as we listen to feedback, both positive and negative.

When someone says, "I really appreciate the work you have been doing for the club," we might notice a tendency either to explain away or brag about our accomplishments. Instead, we can take the opportunity simply to experience fully whatever arises without either minimizing or inflating what we have done.

Do not explain. Our job is to hear how the other person experiences us. We will hear more if we resist the impulse to justify, defend, or explain ourselves.

If someone tells us, "When you were absent from our regular meeting yesterday, I felt angry," our impulse may be to jump in and explain that we went to the funeral of a close friend and that the feedback giver is a major idiot for jumping to conclusions. Instead, we can just listen. Our opportunity to offer feedback can come later.

Many people find it an extremely revealing exercise to take a day to refrain from explaining themselves. It can be shocking to realize how much of the time we unnecessarily explain things in the hope of impressing others in some way or another. Generally, overexplaining tends to have the opposite result: people are put off by it.

Regard all feedback as an offering. Buddhist teachings suggest that we can be grateful to everyone. The point of this outrageous idea is to appreciate the generosity of others, who provide us with the opportunity to learn and develop. If a coworker aggressively attacks us, saying, "I hate it when you give me orders. Who do you think you are anyway? I think you are nothing but a control freak," we might want to cover up our discomfort and embarrassment by immediately attacking back. Instead, we could remind ourselves that it may be very difficult for someone to say this to us and that we could have gone on for years never knowing how another might feel working with us. We can use the situation as an opportunity to develop mindfulness and patience. We can notice how we feel in the moment. We can also contemplate what we have heard. What is of value in it? What can we discard? A later response based on greater clarity may be more skillful than one that immediately responds to aggression with more aggression.

Contemplate what you have heard. We can bring our basic intelligence to what we have heard. We need not assume that the other person's view is more or less accurate than our own. We can practice neither grasping onto nor rejecting what we have heard. Then, we can discover what is useful to us in the feedback. It is not a good idea to quickly change our behavior based on what we have heard.

If we hear something from one person, it might be true and it might not. If we hear it from two people it might still be true or not. If we hear it from three or four or more people, it is probably true.

Recognize your feelings as your own. When we are given feedback, we are likely to have some emotional response to it. The suggestion here is that we recognize that this response is ours; it is not the fault of the other person that we are responding as we are.

When someone gives us negative feedback, we might notice that anger is arising in our minds. We want to blame the other person for making us angry and then avoid making any contact. Or we may recognize that the anger is arising because of our own attachment to being seen in a particular way—for example, as a good and gentle person. By owning our anger and feeling it completely, we open the way for further communication with the person who gave us the feedback.

By working with giving and receiving feedback as an opportunity to cultivate mindfulness, this difficult task can become an interpersonal contemplative practice. When we bring attention to our own discomfort, we can begin to recognize the many ways we all try to hang on to a cherished view of ourselves as solid and separate from others. We can contact the obstacles to the expression of our natural compassion. The ordinary task of telling others how we experience them can become transmuted into compassionate activity that allows us to recognize our connection with others and our essential wakefulness.

Part Five

Taking Action

18
Simple Helping Actions

IN THIS PART OF THE BOOK we will discuss how to take action beyond simply connecting with others. The examples in this chapter were contributed by my students, clients, and colleagues. Before you read this chapter, you might take a moment to ask yourself the question that I have asked the people I know: What has someone done or said that has been helpful to you?

Once we have begun to make some kind of genuine relationship with others by being present with them, listening, and asking clarifying questions, then it might be time to take some kind of action. Sometimes we will already have done enough by just being available and connecting with them. Other times it is appropriate to become more involved.

Each time we offer help to someone it is a unique situation. While there may be some general principles we can follow, in the end we are on our own. This is why it is so important to be as present as we can be. Then our actions can be appropriate to the situation at hand.

Our mindfulness practice helps us be attentive to the details of our moment-to-moment experience as it arises. What naturally happens as we continue our sitting practice is that our mindfulness opens out into what is known as awareness. Where mindfulness is a narrow, single-pointed focus, awareness is broad and panoramic. Mindfulness is like a basketball player knowing how to dribble and shoot baskets. Awareness is like the player knowing where all the other team's players are and how to move in such a way as to get past them. Awareness is bigger than mindfulness and also includes it. The more awareness we have, the better sense we have of what is going on and what might be helpful.

In this chapter, we will look at some simple actions that can be helpful. We can divide these into two broad categories: things we say and things we do.

Helpful Words

Beyond asking questions and giving feedback—which we've already looked at as ways of engaging and connecting with others—there are many ways we can help by talking with others.

First, we can be available. We can invite others to talk or let them know we're available if they need us. Last summer, as my father was in the last days of his life, I got a call from my mother that he was not expected to live much longer. It could be a day or it could be a few days. I held tickets on a flight leaving on Wednesday evening. It was now Tuesday morning. I had a full schedule for the day. I became agitated and confused. Should I go today? How could I reach my husband Fred and let him know if I did? Should I wait for tomorrow? How could I get home and pack—thirty minutes out of town—and then turn around and get to the airport an hour away in the opposite direction? What about my appointments? My mind was racing, my emotions in turmoil. I went into activity. I made phone calls to the airlines. I could get a plane today, but nothing earlier tomorrow than what I already had. I jumped in the car thinking I could find Fred at his usual lunch place. Not there. I stopped at the airlines. Then I slowed down briefly and thought of Louise, the administrative director for the contemplative psychotherapy department. I drove to Naropa. "Louise! I need help!"

She was there. She was calm and just listened to me for a while. She asked a few questions. I began to calm down too. As my mind began to settle, I made a decision to go as soon as possible. Louise said, "I think you have to go," and offered to take care of the dogs and house. As it turned out, I reached Fred and our usual house sitter. I canceled my appointments. Fred and I were on a plane two hours later. I had my last lucid talk with Pop the next morning.

The most important way Louise helped was by being a listening and caring person. It was also very helpful to have someone say, "Yes, go ahead, you can do that."

Sometimes people know that they are having a hard time but are unsure whether to seek out help. We can lend support by being a reality check. In the same way that Louise said, "I think you have to go," we might say, "Yes, this is a real problem, you're quite right to want to call the doctor" (or the pastor, the rabbi, social services, the plumber, or whoever it is). Sometimes we need support to take a step. We may hesitate because we're afraid of making a mistake or an unnecessarily big deal out of something, or because we're concerned that we're just being weak or a kvetch.

Similar to providing a reality check is offering encouragement. We can let people know that we believe they are capable of taking on something that seems a bit daunting. My spiritual teacher, Chögyam Trungpa Rinpoche, often said to his students, "You can do it!" Of course, we should really believe it when we say this.

Encouragement can also be telling someone that they *don't* have to do something. "My therapist told me that I didn't have to atone or make amends by becoming a nurse, which I didn't want to do."

I was part of a therapy team and one day we had a particularly challenging interaction with a very angry client who had thrown a book at me. I was quite shaken, but I believed it was my responsibility as the team's leader to hold things together. The rest of the team cut right through that idea and told me to go home. "You need a break. Get out of here."

Sometimes people want reassurance. I am often asked by clients, students, and others, "Do you think this is a crazy idea?" Or, "Do you think I'm selfish to feel this way?" Sometimes, we can just turn it back to the person. "Do you think it's crazy?" (or selfish, or silly or dumb or whatever). Often others can decide for themselves; other times it's useful to hear our opinion. It is frequently true and easy for me to say, "No, I don't think you're crazy. That's how you feel. I can understand how you might feel like that." Other times I might say, "Yeah, that does seem somewhat selfish. It sounds like you think it might be, too."

Sometimes reassurance can take the form of normalizing things. An example would be to let someone know that it is normal for grieving to take a long time and that it is quite common for it to come in waves long after one expects to be done with it. Whatever emotions we experience are normal. As we have discussed, how we move from feeling our emotions into taking action can be examined further, but all emotions are normal. Offering this kind of reassurance can help others discover maitri.

A near relative of encouragement that is good to avoid is what I call mere cheerleading. Mere cheerleading is encouraging people to do things even when we are doubtful about whether they can do them. It is empty of genuineness and probably does more harm than good. Encouraging a friend to apply for a promotion when he is having trouble doing his present job is probably not doing him any favor.

More difficult is telling the truth when it may be critical. "In undergraduate school, a professor of painting told me I was very talented but lazy. It was the first time I can remember that anyone had been completely honest with me. It was extremely painful and extremely helpful."

Providing information is a simple way to be helpful. Often people ask us if we know of a good doctor, a good car mechanic, a dentist, a place to buy those little things that go into the ends of a corn cob so you don't get butter all over your shirt. Whether it is a big or a little problem, often having good information takes us a long way. We can let others know that we can be called upon in this way by simply saying so. This can be especially helpful to those who are new to our area: new students, new coworkers, new neighbors.

A step beyond providing information is making suggestions and giving advice. We might, for example, offer to help a friend brainstorm some possible courses of action. When we use this problem-solving technique, we list all of the possible ways to proceed that we can think of—no matter how ridiculous. Nothing is rejected. Only after we've come up with a long list do we go on to the next stage. Having used the technique to open things up, we go back over the list and see if anything we've listed can lead us to a creative or useful next step. Once people have made decisions, it is better for us to support them than to keep pestering them to reconsider.

Offering advice is a much stickier business. Unsolicited advice is often regarded as a nuisance. In general it is good to help others decide things for themselves. At the same time, advice and suggestions are sometimes timely and appropriate. I try to ask permission first, although this is not always possible. Saying, "May I offer you a suggestion about that?" can be a way of showing respect.

"A friend told me that confusion is okay; it's just like any other feeling. I had been told throughout my life that I *must* know what I'm doing in the future or have some sort of plan.

So just being able to accept that it's okay to be confused was helpful."

"I was in the Hawaiian islands near Kona. I was angry and had been fighting with my wife. I was kicking the car and generally blowing up. A Japanese gardener saw me and very calmly said, 'I hear you are having a bad day today. I, too, was upset the other day. It will be better. Life is like that. Some days it rains; some days the sun shines.' It woke me up to what a fool I was making of myself, but it also showed me that I was not alone in the universe: someone noticed and cared."

"A friend suggested that I write a letter to my mother who had died a few years earlier. I had some things I wished I'd told her. I know she didn't hear them, but it helped me to put them down on paper."

Perhaps the most useful advice I've ever been given came from a housemate. He practiced meditation, and I didn't. I had just heard of the recent death of my best friend from high school. It was the first time a contemporary of mine had died, and I was feeling anxious and upset. "Karen," he said, "why don't you sit?" It was the beginning of my meditation practice.

Giving advice can be tricky. We may be blamed if things don't work out when our advice is followed. We may be willing to take this risk, but we should be aware of it when we offer our suggestions. In the same way that we begin feedback by talking about ourselves, we can do so when we offer advice. "If I were in your position, I might . . ." That's generally easier to hear than, "You should . . ." Even worse is "You should never . . ."

A peculiar thing I've noticed about advice giving is that people often hear what they need to hear regardless of what we actually say. I have often had the experience of students and clients thanking me for something they've heard me say that has been very helpful to them. When they tell me what they've heard, often I don't recognize it at all. Sometimes they even tell me things I don't agree with. This may also happen with what people find useful in this book!

Now that we've identified some basic approaches, let me hasten to say that we should throw any of them out if something else is more useful in a particular instance.

"I had a friend visiting. He was in the bathtub, carrying on about how no one cared about him and he was going to kill himself. I got really mad. He was completely ignoring that he mattered to me. He'd been going on and on for days about how nothing was worth anything and he was just going to shoot himself. I was scared too. I don't know what happened, but I ended up yelling at him, telling how inconsiderate he was. I told him to go ahead, shoot himself, leave me the big mess to clean up.

"He looked stunned. I think it kind of woke him up. It certainly got his attention. When I realized that I had just blown up and told him to go ahead, I felt like an idiot. But he stopped talking about suicide and later went into a program for vets with PTSD."

This story is a good example of not following most of the guidelines. Instead of being nonaggressive and open in a conventional sense, this person blamed her friend and offered no sympathy. She encouraged him to harm himself. Yet she was completely genuine. Clearly this is not something that could be applied indiscriminately. It arose from the moment, and, apparently, was just what was needed.

The most important thing is to actually help. A friend's mother has the following slogan: You're only a help if you're a help. It doesn't matter if we do it right if we are not really helping. Helping is often a messy and uncertain business, involving risks.

Helpful Deeds

Those are some ways of helping by what we say. Now, let's look at some things we can do. When we offer to help, it is better to offer something specific rather than a blanket, "Let me know if I can help." Most people are hesitant to follow up on such a general invitation.

When a person is in bed recovering from illness, surgery, or childbirth, we can offer to mind the children, shop for groceries, run errands, clean the house, drive someone somewhere. We can also cheer them with silly, friendly gifts like a woman who gave a pair of purple earrings to a friend who was recuperating from breast surgery.

"When Jerry was in the hospital, Barry fixed our fence. The latch was broken and the dogs were getting out. I'll never forget that he did that." "When I was called out of town suddenly, Pat made a bunch of phone calls for me. She canceled all my business commitments and explained what was happening to my friends."

When I've asked people what's been helpful to them, the most frequent answer I've gotten was someone giving them a hug. "I received a hug this morning, for no apparent reason, from my girlfriend." "When they were taking Jim away in the ambulance, Tom gave me a hug. He said, 'I didn't know what else to give you.' It was a perfect gift."

Helping clean up the environment can be a big help when people are feeling confused or distressed. Our minds tend to follow our bodies and the environment. If we are in a confused and messy place, it is harder to be clear. When people have a lot to do already, we can help by offering to tidy up or do a load of laundry. When people are agitated, partly because there is no way they can be helpful themselves, we can invite them to clean up with us. Getting people to pay attention to details of sweeping the floor or putting away the dishes can help them bring body and mind together. This helps mind to slow down and can be a big relief. It is an invitation to be mindful and grounded.

Having the environment clean and welcoming goes a very long way. If we are in a situation where it is appropriate, we can bring in fresh flowers, keep things uncluttered, and offer good food and drink.

One creative gift a woman gave her partner helped him create a good environment for himself when he took a difficult trip. Darrin described this gift appreciatively. "Just before I took a trip to New York City to see my family for the first time in six years, my partner gave me a care package filled with lavender oil for aromatherapy, bath salts for my body to relax into, photos of happy, loving times, a book of inspiring thoughts, and candy for sweetness."

A very ordinary thing we can do to help is to teach or show someone else how to do something. "I had a client once who for some reason had never been taught how to tie his shoes. He nearly always wore slip-ons. He badly needed to enter a drug treatment program. It turned out what scared him most was having to attend the physical education classes, because he would have to reveal that he couldn't tie his own sneakers. I taught him how to tie his shoes."

When we teach people things we can be sensitive to the feelings that can arise for others. Like the man who couldn't tie his shoes, sometimes people feel embarrassed or ashamed of their lack of know-how. Instead of saying, "What, you don't know how to tie your shoes? How did you miss out on learning such a simple thing!" we could support the intelligence and courage this man showed in revealing his secret failing. "Great, you've come this far, now we can go farther. Let me show you how to do the next step."

Sometimes simple helping actions occur in response to emergency situations.

"I was driving down Broadway and stopped for a red light. There were two cars in front of me. When the light changed, the first car didn't go. The one in front of me went around it. I could see the driver of the first car kind of thrashing around. I got out of my car and into his, pushed him over to the passenger seat, and drove his car into a parking lot. A woman I'd never seen before saw what I did and asked if she could help. I asked her to call an ambulance. Then I got my car out of the street. When the ambulance came, it turned out that the man had had a stroke. When they left, this woman and I—total strangers, one Hispanic and one Anglo—gave each other a big hug and wept together. It was a sweet heart connection."

Making a phone call, driving a car. These are very simple things, but they may have saved a life. I am always touched when I hear stories of people coming forward to help strangers. An interesting study done in New York City revealed that even in this large city people will come forward to help. A researcher pretended to be ill on a New York subway car to see what people would do. In nearly every instance he was helped. Even when he seemed to be drunk he was helped half of the time.

Of course, it is also possible to be a big nuisance. If we rush in to help without really paying attention, we can make things worse. When Jim was having a heart attack and people were all waiting for the ambulance, one of the women present said, "Let's all make a circle and hold hands and give good energy to Jim." That might have been just right for someone else, but not for Jim. He hated it. It would have been better to check out whether this would have been comforting first.

Another kind of problem we should avoid is idiot compassion, which is being nice to people because it is easier to be agreeable than it is to be genuinely helpful. We fall into idiot compassion when we do things that we tell ourselves are meant to remove the other person's pain, but are really the result of our confusion. They are often stopgap measures that alleviate an immediate need but are actually harmful in the long run. Offering drugs to relieve the pain of an addict beginning to enter withdrawal is an example of idiot compassion.

When we make a mistake, the best thing is to admit it and stop doing whatever it is. Our meditation practice is a big support for helping us practice letting go. We only make things worse if we persist in something that is not helpful.

Sometimes we might think being a help takes a lot of specialized training. Sometimes it does, but more often all it takes to provide help is paying attention and being willing to get involved. Then, many times, the most simple things are the most helpful.

19 Untapped Resources

AS WE DISCUSSED IN CHAPTER 10, we are all quite skilled at becoming mindless, losing track of the present moment by indulging in mindlessness practices that disconnect our bodies and minds. These very same mindlessness practices are often a source of wealth to us as helpers.

There are three main ways in which mindlessness practices are useful. First, they can be the basis of mindfulness; second, they can provide alternatives to more harmful mindlessness practices; third, they can be used as a way to pace ourselves so that we do not fall into pointless and self-aggressive ambition. They provide assets for us as helpers if we understand these different uses.

As we have already seen, mindlessness practices come in a myriad of forms. They range from overt physical practices like hair-twirling, chalk-rolling, and doodling, to invisible activities like obsessing or fantasizing. When we are caught up in mindlessness practices, we tend to be irritated if we are interrupted, and we are often out of touch with our compassionate hearts.

Transforming Mindlessness into Mindfulness

Things that are generally regarded as mindfulness practices can be coopted and turned into mindlessness practices if they are used to desynchronize body and mind instead of bringing them together in the present moment. Yoga and t'ai chi, or even sitting practice, can be so misused. It all depends on what kind of intention and effort we bring to them. If, for example, we sit down on our cushion and use the time to spin out fantasies in an effort to escape our present situation, ignoring the moments when we momentarily wake up, then we have turned our practice into a mindless one. If we put on music while we do our yoga so that we can get swept up and away, we distort our practice.

On the other hand, we can take seemingly mindless activities and transform them into opportunities to bring ourselves into nowness if we bring our curiosity and attention to them. Often people think that we need to stop doing the mindlessness practice in order for it to be useful to us. However, that's not quite it. We can become interested in all of the details of what we are already doing and that in itself can be mindfulness. If we stop the activity, we'll never find out about it.

My favorite mindlessness practice for highlighting this possibility is nail biting. We can get interested in all of the details involved in it. When do we do it? How do we select which finger to begin with? How do we know when to go on to another nail? Where are our minds? What happens to our relationships with others when we are engaged in it? How often do we do it? How do we know when to stop? Some nail biters have told me that they stop when they hurt themselves. They are suddenly back in the present moment since the pain has brought their minds and bodies together. Before that they might have been lost in thought or in a kind of half-present state, only partially noticing what was happening around them.

When we as helpers become interested in what others do when they engage in mindlessness practices, it invites them to begin to notice, too. Sometimes our interest may be annoying. We have to have some sensitivity about this since we might be regarded as interruptions (and hence as irritants). But if we can bring curiosity, and maybe humor, to our exploration with people of what they are doing, it may shift the allegiance of the practice toward wakefulness.

We can all learn to use mindlessness practices as reminders to wake up. When we find that we are playing with paper clips or drumming our fingers, we can let that bring us into the present moment. When I am working with clients, I've noticed that if I'm sitting on the edge of my seat I've probably gotten caught up in my own mind and have begun to stop hearing the client. I'm just waiting until I can interject my "brilliant insight." When I notice that my posture has shifted in this way, I practice touch and go. I note what I'm doing, feeling, and thinking, and then let it go and come back to the client and the room. This mindless behavior has become a reminder for me to wake up.

Reducing Harm

The second way that we can make use of mindlessness practices is by using less harmful practices to replace harmful ones. All mindlessness practices are somewhat problematic, but some are better than others.

A woman I knew had a mindless obsessing practice. She would go over and over the accident that killed her fiancé. She would think of all the ways she might have prevented the accident. "If only I had gone with him that day . . . if only I had called him . . . if only we hadn't had that argument." And on and on. It is easy to fall into this kind of "if only" practice. It seems to take us away from the pain of the present moment, but it keeps us from letting it go as well. Ironically, it is a way of becoming stuck in the pain since the "if only's" are painful in themselves.

She also obsessively went over her fantasies about what the last moments of her lover's life must have been like. She would imagine his terror as the oncoming car approached. She would get lost in the pain she imagined he felt. This was extremely painful for her. Once she took a load of sleeping pills and was prevented from dying by her dogs waking her up. Once awakened, she got help, but she can still find herself thinking suicidal thoughts.

This woman found that she was better able to cope when she practiced touch and go with her grief or with the helplessness she felt when she thought of her lover's death. By bringing her attention to how she felt when she indulged in her mindlessness practice, she came into the present moment. The automatic quality of becoming lost in her thoughts became undermined. She learned to turn to a less harmful practice: reading science fiction novels.

Addictions can be regarded as mindlessness practices. They desynchronize the mind and the body and often also produce states of mind that are hazy or even delusional. They are especially insidious since the body becomes dependent upon whatever substance is being employed. Alcohol and drug addictions can be harmful not only to one's own health but also to the well-being of others. Alcohol especially is linked with increased violence and fatal accidents. Addictive practices can be quite complex, and people often require professional help or the support of self-help groups like twelve-step groups. As part of the recovery process, replacing a drug or alcohol addiction with a less harmful mindlessness practice can be quite beneficial. Sometimes recovering addicts find that they can use jogging or other sports fruitfully. Mindlessly running with music playing over headphones can be a good activity compared with the harm of substance abuse.

Finding a Middle Way

Not only can we substitute less dangerous patterns for more dangerous ones, we can use mindlessness practices as a way of moderating the intensity of our experience and as a way of staying on the path. This is the third use of these practices.

In Buddhism we talk of a gradual path toward waking up. The idea is that we cannot do it all at once. As we have seen many times, having maitri means that we are realistic and friendly toward ourselves. Rather than falling into the extremes of pushing ourselves aggressively or of doing nothing at all, we try to find the middle way. In this balancing act, we can use mindlessness practices in a mindful way.

We may have the overall aspiration to wake up, yet sometimes we feel unable to be fully present. Perhaps the pain of a situation is particularly intense: Dick is in the hospital after collapsing. He will be there for a few days while tests are run. Fran, his wife, will have no news for days. Her tendency is to fall into mindless worrying. Toni works in a very high-pressured business environment. She feels that she has to be "on" all the time. She wants some down time when she comes home, but her partner greets her with the news that little Johnny's teacher is upset with his behavior at school. She turns angrily to Johnny with her hand raised.

In both these examples, we see people about to fall into mindless behavior: worrying and hitting. Both of these might be harmful. Fran has high blood pressure and the stress of the situation may escalate as she imagines all of the possible terrible scenarios she can come up with. Toni might actually harm her child; if she hits him, she will certainly frighten him and damage his feeling of safety. She may also teach him that hitting is an acceptable way to deal with things.

It would be better if Fran could do something else that engages her attention. A mindless activity like losing herself in a movie may help her be more present later when she is needed. If Toni can sit down in front of the television for a half an hour, she may wind down enough to access her tender heart later.

I met a woman in Australia who had a computer game practice. A very busy attorney, she would come home every day and play this game. While she played it, her children would talk to her. Her kids loved this time of day. She was more present playing the computer game than she would be if she just sailed in from work and talked to them. I have to admit I was unprepared for this! When she started to speak I had expected that this would turn out to be a great mindlessness practice that would cut her off from her kids, but I was wrong. Instead, it was a middle-way practice that let her become more present and less mindless.

When we seek to help others it is good to keep our eyes open for mindlessness practices that can be used in these ways. Sometimes we can invite others to join us or suggest activities to them.

"I was very depressed and lonely about my marriage breaking up. A good friend took me out and played video poker with me. He didn't make a big deal about it, but I felt like someone cared about me. It got my mind off of things."

I have known several women who use ironing as a middle-way practice. When one of them felt anxious, her old practice would have been to reach for a drink. Instead, she realized that ironing was also a way to calm down. Sometimes it was a mindfulness practice, and other times it wasn't. It didn't seem to matter very much what she ironed.

Choosing to do a mindlessness practice on purpose can give one a sense of empowerment. Instead of feeling swept away by the speed of one's mind and the momentum of habitual activities, one can make a choice. This in itself can be helpful. If our overall intentions are to develop mindfulness of the present moment and to cultivate maitri, both in ourselves and in others, mindlessness practices are a rich resource.

20 Mindful Companionship

SOMETIMES WE NEED TO DO MORE than perform the kind of simple actions we discussed in chapter 18. Often others need us to provide more of an ongoing presence. They may need us to help in a particular task, such as decision-making, or they may need continuing assistance when they are ill or dying. In contemplative psychotherapy there is a technique called "basic attendance" that refers to attentively accompanying others in order to support them, to help them become more mindful, and to invite them into social interaction. This technique has been used with success with different kinds of people, including those with psychotic disorders and the elderly. A therapist who practices basic attendance is sometimes called a therapist-friend. It is a style of helping that can have many applications for all of us.

"My husband's brother had some kind of a breakdown years ago. No one knew what to do with him, so they sent him to stay with us. He and I planted tomatoes, went grocery shopping, and just did ordinary things."

This woman, quite naturally, discovered the heart of basic attendance: doing ordinary things together that invite the people being attended to notice the environment and their own perceptions in the context of a caring, genuine relationship.

"When I was in college, I broke up with my boyfriend. Or, rather, he broke up with me. It was unexpected and overwhelming. My roommate took me home with her over the winter break. I was a mess: moping around, getting lost in memories, and planning how I could get him back. He was the only thing I could talk about. I'm sure I must have been driving her nuts. Somehow she got me interested in playing the guitar. When I was playing, I had to pay attention to what I was doing. And singing along with it, I had to really breathe. It got me out of my swamp of self-pity. It was really generous of her. I don't know which was harder: listening to me carrying on about my boyfriend or listening to me clumsily playing the same song over and over, one chord at a time."

When we ask people to come for a walk, or to put in a garden, or to do the housework, we can practice basic attendance. What this means, first of all, is that we are being mindfully present. We pay attention to our own experience, our sense perceptions, feelings, and thoughts. We notice the exchange and practice touch and go with it.

Helping Others Develop Mindfulness

We might invite the people we attend to pay attention to their experiences as well. I once worked with a man who suffered from debilitating auditory hallucinations. When the voices came, he couldn't tell what was in his mind and what came from outside. He once told me, "You know, when I'm confused about what is real and what's not, it doesn't help me at all to try to get me to sort it all out. What helps is if someone says, 'Larry, would you like a Coke?' " Offering a Coke or a glass of water or a baseball to people who are lost in their own preoccupations can invite them to pay attention to the present moment.

In doing basic attendance with others we can invite them to engage in an activity that helps join mind and body. When we do this we can help others to transform ordinary activities into mindfulness practices.

"Darrin helped me bring in water and wood, not only because I wasn't feeling up to it, but to get me to participate. It got me out of my head. Then he commented on the view and the feel of the air to remind me to touch in to my feelings."

Using everyday activities as opportunities to cultivate mindfulness and maitri is a basic principle of contemplative psychotherapy. There are innumerable things that we all do that can be transformed in this way. Many physical activities, such as engaging in sports, getting dressed and putting on makeup, washing the car, or playing a musical instrument, can become mindfulness practices. Working often provides many opportunities to develop mindfulness. For example, waiting on tables in restaurants requires tremendous attention to detail as well as an overall sense of the environment. Good servers can see what is going to be needed before the diner asks for it.

A truly mindful activity has four special qualities. The more of these four qualities a pastime has, the more potential it has to cultivate mindfulness. The first of these qualities is that it brings mind and body together. Instead of being lost in the past or the future, mind is present right here in the body. Our bodies are always in the present, so if we can bring our attention to them, they can provide an anchor in the present moment. The second quality is that it gives us the opportunity to practice touch and go. Not only do we experience our sense perceptions and our bodily feelings, we also notice what is going on emotionally. Then, we note our experience and go on to the next moment.

When I play the piano, I can practice touch and go. If I get caught up in trying to get it exactly right, I can feel the tension in my body and in my mind. Usually I mess up the next passage when I do that. If I can simply notice the strong desire as it arises and let it come and go, then I can stay with the music as it goes along. Finding the balance between too tight and too loose applies to any mindfulness practice, whether it's sitting meditation or playing the piano.

The third quality of mindfulness is that the activity lets us notice when we come back to the present moment after being lost in our minds. Driving along the highway we might notice that we've been gone for the last while. Coming back, we can notice that we're back again, like a client of mine who drove every day between Boulder and Denver—about twenty-five miles. She cultivated what she called "driving practice" from when she got on the entrance ramp in Denver until she came off the highway in Boulder. This practice highlighted for her the difference between being present and not being present. Another way of describing this quality is to say that the activity illuminates a sense of contrast.

The fourth quality is being present with each changing moment of nowness. Each moment is fresh and unique, and a good mindfulness practice shows this to us again and again. Recognizing new moments as they arise lets us discover that everything is always changing, including us.

Any activity that brings all four of these together will help us become more mindful. As basic attendants we can support the mindfulness of others by paying attention to the activities in their lives that can be cultivated as mindfulness practices. We do this first by being curious about what people do. We can do it with them or we can listen as they tell us. The more detail they can give us, the more attentive they will become themselves. Then, we can also inquire about the four qualities.

A client of mine told me she was a rock climber. Her rock climbing brought her sharply into her body. She needed to know exactly where each limb was, and she needed to use her sight, hearing, and sense of touch to find the next hold. She had to be precise about how she shifted her weight and about listening to the others with whom she climbed. When fear would arise, she could feel it and let it go again. I was very curious about how she came back to the present moment when she became lost in thoughts. Even though she could not describe what she did, she knew how to do it. The fourth quality of being present with each changing moment was also very much part of climbing. Our conversations about climbing made her more aware of what she already knew, and she then was able to apply her mindfulness in other areas of her life.

Nearly everyone has something that can be worked with in this way. If all four qualities are not present in any particular activity, we can become interested in how they might be developed. When we teach students basic counseling skills, sometimes we ask them to do ten-minute practice interviews in groups of three. One person is the client, another is the therapist, and the third is the mindfulness coach. The job of the mindfulness coach is to ask each of the others to describe their experiences at the halfway point and at the end of the practice exercise. As mindful companions we too can serve as mindfulness coaches.

Another thing we can do as mindful companions is work with others' mindlessness practices. We can help them transform their mindlessness practices into mindfulness practices, or we can support them in replacing a harmful practice with a more benign one, as we discussed in the last chapter.

Assisting Others in Decision-Making

As people become grounded in the present moment, we can become helpful in directing their attention to what to do next. In cultivating our own sanity, we have learned to appreciate the richness of our experience and have practiced clarifying our understanding and our intentions. We can help others through these two stages too. Helping people come into the present moment is inviting them to appreciate their wealth. Assisting them in setting priorities, identifying immediate and long-term goals, and clarifying their intentions is helping them practice clear seeing.

As we assist others in decision-making about their next steps, we can inquire as to what resources they have to draw on, what they have already tried, and what has worked for them before. We can help them decide what needs to be done first and what can be put aside for now. If we stick to what can be done and follow through on it, confidence will naturally develop. If we set unreasonable goals and then, naturally, fail at meeting them, our confidence will diminish. This is a good principle to keep in mind for ourselves and for those we are helping.

Sometimes people want our help as they sort out what kind of help they themselves want to offer to others. We can share what we know about how this process can work. We can help them attend to all aspects of the cycle of helping, especially if we can assist them in touching in with themselves before extending out to others.

A mistake we can make is to join others in a complaint session. Of course, we can listen and be supportive. But jumping in and wallowing around, endorsing the belief that everything is hopeless and nothing will do any good, will only encourage depression and inaction. It is generally more helpful to support what is healthy in the person. On the other hand, we shouldn't be Pollyannas who regard things in the rosy glow of self-deception.

Basic Attendance with the Elderly, the Ill, and the Dying

An important application of basic attendance is how we interact with the elderly. As we grow older, we lose some of the abilities we had when we were younger. Research suggests that most of us keep many of our mental abilities with the exception of our short-term memories. Physically, though, we slow down, lose strength and balance, and have many more ailments. When we help the elderly it is important not to fall into the mistake of treating them as children. This can be painfully insulting to our elders. Instead, we can bring a sense of respect.

A colleague of mine, Victoria Howard, who specializes in working with basic attendance and the elderly, suggests that a particularly important time to be helpful is in transitions. When people are waking up, they may feel confused and vulnerable. A steady mindful presence can be very helpful. Getting ready to leave the house can take longer than it used to. Feeling the patience of one's companion can be a relief.

Vicki points out that many elderly people are extremely generous in their willingness to let us into their lives and in their desire to pass on what they have learned to the next generation. The intention to offer the transmission of our wisdom arises for most of us as we age. Sometimes this transmission can involve an important body of knowledge. Other times it may seem trivial, like telling a youngster the right way to write a thank-you note, detail by painful detail. If we can recognize the wisdom in such transmissions, we can be much more present and appreciative than if we try to get the elder to go at our younger pace or tell them we already know all about thank-you notes.

In helping the ill or the dying, basic attendance is sometimes the most important thing we can do. As we've noted earlier, our minds tend to reflect and exchange with what is happening in the environment and the people in it. Bringing a quality of mindfulness to our minds and a sense of peacefulness and upliftedness to the environment can be extremely helpful to those who are distressed or ill.

Providing an environment of calm and ordinariness can be a real gift. As we work with our minds and return again and again to the present moment, we can notice small things that we can do. These might include holding the basin for someone who needs to vomit, fixing the pillow, holding a glass of water with a bent straw, or offering to read aloud. The most important thing is that we let ourselves be as present as we can. Out of that we will have a better sense of what might be helpful right now. We can listen carefully to what others say about what they want or how they feel.

If the people we are involved with are in a nursing home or a hospital, we might imagine what that is like for them. Do they feel hopeless? In pain? As if they're being treated disrespectfully? Frightened? If we let ourselves experience the exchange and also use our imaginations, we can let our hearts be touched. Out of that ground of compassion, our actions can be more helpful. Perhaps we can talk to the health-care workers on the person's behalf or help keep arguing visitors out of the room.

"When my mother was dying and in and out of a coma, the visiting nurse and the nurse's aide got into a big argument about who should have brought the new bottle of medicine. They just ignored my mother, who was lying there. It made me so angry, but I got them out of the room. Then, I worked with my own mind until I could bring something other than anger back in."

When there is nothing overt we can do, we can sit by the person and practice tonglen. We can breathe in the person's fear and pain and breathe out to them a sense of confidence and peacefulness—or whatever arises for us as we practice. Practicing in this way can help us stay in the moment and not spin out into our own fears and fantasies. It may also bring the qualities of workability and of warmth into the environment.

In the final ten minutes of my father's life, I sat by his bed and practiced tonglen. I told the nurse's aide that I was trying to breathe in his pain and breathe out a sense of peace. I told her I could use some support, meaning that I could use some comfort myself. I still hold the vivid memory of her hand and my mine clasping as we reached out toward each other. I found out later that she too had practiced tonglen based on the little I had said. My father died in that very quiet and calm environment. I will always be grateful for her kindness.

There are an endless number of situations in which we can practice basic attendance. We might attend to a friend, a colleague, an elderly relative, our child, a client. If we can bring a mindful, steady presence to the situation, we can give others the message that they are basically good and that things are fundamentally workable. By working with the details of the environment, the cultivation of others' mindfulness where possible, and the warmth of genuine contact, we may find that we, too, develop more mindfulness and compassion.

21
Teamwork

SOME OF US REMEMBER TIMES when the neighborhood, or the extended family, was a kind of small tribe that came together to offer help in times of need: raising a barn, throwing a party to raise rent money, keeping an eye on everyone's children, tending the ill and the dying. In some places various groups and congregations still perform similar functions. In other situations, we find ourselves far from family, and it is a group of friends who become involved when the need for help arises.

I've known several couples who called upon their friends to take care of special tasks for their weddings. They asked some to serve as ushers at the event, some to transport family members from the airport to the hotel and then to the wedding and reception, some to serve refreshments to the family and minister before the ceremony, and still others to take care of the millions of details a wedding can entail.

When such helpers pay attention not only to the details of their tasks, but also to creating an environment of sanity and upliftedness, they become a basic attendance team. Working not only with the outer environment, but also with their own minds, they can bring a grounded quality that helps everyone involved.

I once participated in a wedding where the bride's parents, who had been divorced for many years, were both in attendance. Their friction blew up just before the ceremony was scheduled to begin, and the bride became very upset. She and her fiancé had done a good job of surrounding themselves with a group of supportive and mindful friends. Two friends saw to it that the parents were gently separated and seated far apart. Another sat down with the bride and helped her calm down by being calm herself. Simple things like getting water, providing tissues, and acknowledging how much pain the bride was feeling helped her to touch her feelings and also to let go of them. She recognized her unrealistic dream of having everybody get along (as they never did anywhere else) and shifted her attention to the important meaning of this day: she was making an important commitment and it was worthy of celebration.

Other weddings have been less explosive, but nonetheless this nervous-making, joyful day can benefit from the creation of a strong container of sanity. In some Buddhist centers, when a wedding is held the guests are invited to come an hour early and practice sitting meditation. The idea is to create an environment based on mindfulness and awareness into which the wedding party can come.

Creating a container of mindfulness and maitri can be helpful in many settings. I've seen teams of helpers bring the principles of basic attendance into assisting childbirth, elder-care, and attending the injured, the ill, and the dying. Sometimes these teams have been only loosely knit together; other times they have been well organized and have had team leaders.

As we become more at home in applying the principles of basic attendance—being present, creating an environment of mindfulness and maitri, attending to the environment, inviting others to become mindful, and nurturing the development of maitri—we can teach what we know to others. This can be a gift to one's family and friends.

Clark had been doing sitting meditation practice for a number of years and had some experience in basic attendance. He went to visit his parents when his father's cancer had became advanced enough to send him to bed. Because Clark was listening well, he recognized an indirect invitation from his father to talk about death. "I think," said his father, speaking very slowly, "Jack Kevorkian [the suicide doctor] has the right idea."

Instead of saying something like, "Now, now, you mustn't think like that," or becoming upset by this display of "hopelessness," Clark said, "It sounds like you're getting ready to die."

His father was quiet for a minute or so, and then said, "Yes. That's right." "Are you afraid?" Clark asked. "No. I'm not afraid of dying, but I am afraid of spending the rest of my life helpless and in pain."

The conversation went on, with many long pauses, from there. In the silences, Clark did his best to remain present and open.

His sister-in-law said, "Clark's talk with Dad opened the door for the rest of us to be more honest about what was happening. We'd all been tiptoeing around, afraid to show Dad that we thought he was dying. It was a big relief to everybody." Later, when the dying man refused treatment for an ancillary infection, no one argued.

Clark was able to tell, and show, his brother and sister-in-law what he knew about creating an environment of mindfulness. For many people, it can be a relief to have death talked about openly. Otherwise, while the family is putting on a brave front, the dying person feels more and more isolated and cut off. He doesn't want to upset anyone by talking about his dying, but it is very much on his mind. For others, of course, it might not be a good idea to address dying directly. As usual, no one guideline applies to everyone.

With Clark's father, the team was made up of family members and also hospice workers. There was no one really in charge on the spot, but there was a group understanding that creating a peaceful environment at home, with medical support for his physical comfort, was the best thing they could do to help his Dad as he died.

I've had several friends gather teams of friends and professionals to help when they had babies. One woman had her baby at home; two others had friends come and help at the hospital. The helpers did their best to create a mindful atmosphere. They attended to details like offering ice chips, holding the mother's legs as she had contractions, wiping her forehead. One of the new fathers reported, "I don't know how people go through this alone!" These teams of helping friends came together, attending mindfully to whatever needed doing. They are good examples of teams without leaders.

In contemplative psychotherapy one important style of working with others is the use of teams that provide basic attendance. These teams have leaders who attend to the overall well-being of all the team's members, as well as the person who is the identified client. Such teams have worked for many years in a variety of settings, both private and public, with different kinds of people. This approach has been used most in working with the elderly and with those suffering from major mental illnesses, often providing an alternative to institutionalized care.

Having a team of helping friends with a team leader, or several team leaders, has also been used in nonprofessional settings.

Alan was diagnosed with melanoma a few years ago. For a period of months he followed a particular treatment approach calling for a special diet requiring pure water and organic vegetables. It took a great deal of work to prepare all the meals.

Alan and his wife, Ann, found that many of their friends wanted to help. One friend, Kathy, offered to coordinate some of their efforts.

As Kathy has since described it, she felt inspired to become involved. "If we could gather a community of people who cared for them it would be healing for Alan. It could be powerful, magical. So, I offered."

She met with both Ann and Alan and talked about what would be useful to them. Ann gave Kathy a list of people who had offered to help and she contacted them. There was a lot to do: equipment to be gathered for the special diet, vegetables to be chopped, juices made, meals put together. Kathy, often at home with her two-year-old daughter, made a lot of phone calls. She kept a file of relevant information and notes. She met with Ann about every other week, and they had numerous phone conversations in between.

Kathy's husband, Jamie, was also very involved. He often did basic attendance "shifts" for the household. Sometimes he would prepare vegetables or shop for organic foods. Sometimes he just spent time with Alan, watching television and talking about cars. Other times they would talk of Alan's family and his fears.

After a few months it became clear that the cancer was spreading and that Alan was going to die. By this time Kathy needed to stay home with her daughter, and some others stepped into different team leadership roles. One friend coordinated a group who prepared meals at their own homes and brought them over. Other friends took on sorting out other tasks as they arose: working out timetables with the mortuary, inquiring about death certificates, arranging for family members to be hosted in various ways before, during, and after the funeral.

As the end drew nearer, Ann and Alan met with a close friend, Antonio, whom Alan had requested to conduct the funeral service. He was a steady presence, answering questions and helping them plan the service.

Shari, one of the friends who had taken on more of the team leadership role toward the end, coordinated a small group of people who took turns staying overnight and doing basic attendance shifts. They did whatever was needed. Sometimes Shari would talk with Ann; sometimes she washed the dishes.

As Alan became less available, Shari found that sometimes her job was to tell people that they couldn't see him. When she remembers that time, she thinks of "both the brilliance and the confusion of the situation. They were both heightened. I found myself attending to the attendants, especially as they felt further away from Alan. Sometimes people felt confused or irritated. I found myself laughing more toward the end. There was no way to please everybody and no way to control things."

In the last two weeks Jamie organized people into basic attendance shifts to the household since Alan was going to die at home. This often meant talking with them about dying and letting them know what they were coming into. People came to create a container of mindfulness and compassionate love.

One of the friends who came to do basic attendance shifts has commented on "Ann and Alan's generosity and hospitality to us. They let others in to partake of the situation. It was spooky because it was so ordinary. When I would go into the environment, there was a quality of appreciation, of friendship, and of utter sadness all linked together. Maybe it was more helpful to us. To connect with the reality of dying was really quite a gift. It's an experience you take with you."

As Alan spent less time awake, the team members practiced sitting meditation and tonglen practice around the clock, often sitting near his bed. After Alan died, people continued to sit in shifts with his body until the funeral service. He was forty-four.

Shari recalls, "The most amazing thing was being with Alan when he was dying. I'd never done that before. It changed my life. I've felt different about dying ever since. It's like, 'Oh, I can do this. This is human and ordinary at the end.' Something dropped away. It really helped me somehow to be there. It felt like Alan's generosity."

As the person coordinating the scheduling of the shifts, Jamie was often the person to deal with Alan's friends' reactions to his dying. Some were shocked, and Jamie needed to be gentle and kind with them. When Jamie thinks back on his experience he sums it up saying, "There was a definite quality of sharing the environment of Alan's generosity, and an experience of deep friendship." Then he adds, "It was also really awful and painful."

Looking back on this time, Ann says, "Having a support team for ten months during Alan's illness gave us stability, a container of support to which we could reach out when we needed help. It was a community of friends who honored and respected us. This was the ground of each relationship and was healing in itself.

"Early on, the focus was on helping by doing all the many things that took energy that we didn't have. It was enormously helpful and allowed us to maintain some steadiness and balance while undergoing an extremely rigorous regime of nutritional treatment.

"During the five months before Alan died, the focus was on helping by being. To have the companionship of trusted friends who were willing to be ordinary with us while we moved closer to death was a precious gift. It was ordinary and extraordinary at the same time."

The various team leaders coordinated the efforts of a large group of people. As much as possible they relieved the burdens of Ann and Alan. In addition, they attended to the helpers. This, too, is part of the team leader role.

In contemplative psychotherapy the recognition that everyone in the situation is being helped is called "mutual recovery."

Whether we are the identified recipients of help or the designated givers of help, we all benefit from the practices of mindfulness and maitri, and we all have the opportunity to be generous.

The application of the basic attendance team approach could be applied creatively to many situations. The important point is simply to take care of what needs attention in both the outer environment and our own minds.

22
Body-Speech-Mind Groups

THOSE OF US WHOSE WORK ENTAILS helping others on a regular basis usually find that we need support and help ourselves. In particular, we may want assistance in working with the experience of exchange. As we've discussed, exchange is the naturally occurring phenomenon of connecting directly with others. Health professionals often carry home with them a load of painful emotions that they've picked up during the day. The rest of us may also find that despite practicing touch and go, we have collected a residue of pain that we don't know what to do with. Of course, we can do a lot by carrying on with our sitting practices of mindfulness-awareness and tonglen. In contemplative psychotherapy, we supplement our individual practices with a style of presenting our work called body-speech-mind, which focuses especially on working with exchange.

This kind of presentation can be useful to all kinds of helpers in several different ways. Sometimes we feel stuck in the exchange, as if we're carrying feelings that are not our own but that we can't seem to shake. It can also help us clarify what is going on in our relationship with someone when we are feeling unsure or confused. And finally, it is a good way to reconnect with our hearts when we have begun to shut down out of fatigue, frustration, or distaste. Paradoxically, the more we can open to the exchange and allow ourselves to really feel the predicament of the other person, the more we are able to let go as well. Our hearts become more raw and exposed and we have a better sense of how to proceed.

The body-speech-mind practice is a group practice. In the same way that teams of helpers can bring together a variety of viewpoints and talents, groups of helpers gathering to help each other can provide a quality of freshness and diversity that we cannot tap on our own. For people who work professionally as helpers—teachers, therapists, physicians, nurses, and so on—groups of colleagues can gather. For the many others who are helpers without formal credentials, any group of interested people could work. We have seen such groups work especially well if all the participants have a mindfulness-awareness sitting practice, but it has also been useful when only one or two of the people have a practice. These groups are themselves an opportunity to practice being present and working with what arises.

What are these groups and how do they work? The aim of any body-speech-mind group session is to invite the relationship of the helper and the one being helped into the room. One important guideline that has proven its worth over time is assuming that everything that arises for anyone in the group is relevant to this relationship. For example, if I am feeling antsy or bored, that is regarded as useful information about the presentation. If I start to feel spaced out or angry or sad, it may be valuable to share that.

Our job as listeners is to let the presenter know what we are experiencing as the presentation goes along, so we need to track our own experience. Our job as presenters is to introduce our "client" to the other group members. Although most of us are helping friends, colleagues, family, and other assorted noncategorizable people, for convenience I will call them all clients throughout this description.

Clients are not actually in the room, but we try to bring them there by precisely describing the details of their body, speech, and mind. We evoke their presence by paying close attention to all we know about them as they are right now. We do not include much history, unless it is vitally important to our understanding of the person's present situation. We try our best to describe and not interpret. This is another important guideline. So, for example, I wouldn't start by saying, "Bill is a really paranoid kind of guy who is driving me crazy." Instead, I would start by simply bringing Bill into the room by telling the others what he looks like. I might begin by saying, "Bill is about thirty-seven years old; he has dark brown hair that he combs back from his forehead. His hair is always clean and shining. It's shorter on the sides and his ears show."

As much as possible, we keep our opinions out of it. We are trying to see as clearly as we can who Bill is, not what we think of him. After all, it may be our own opinions and expectations that keep us from exchanging completely. Sticking to the discipline of description instead of interpretation takes some practice, and this is where the group members can help each other. A group member might ask, for example, "What is it that Bill does with his face that makes you want to say that he 'scowls disdainfully'?" Then the presenter can be more descriptive.

Body

In describing body, we spend lots of time on the details of appearance: hair, face, skin tone, ears, teeth, eyebrows, body weight, muscle tone, shape, and so on. Nothing is too trivial for us to include. The more the better. Sometimes it might seem a bit tedious, but we have found that the more precise we can be, the more the person starts to come alive for us. What does his nose look like? How about his hands? Does he wear jewelry? Does he bite his nails? How does he dress? What colors does he like to wear? What kind of shoes does he have? What is his posture like? Does he walk tall? Slump? How does he sit? Can the presenter show us?

We are often surprised to realize how little we remember! That's okay too. Whatever we don't remember, we just say so. If nothing else happens, we can become aware of how much we have been absent with this person, and next time we will find that we look at him differently.

We include anything that has a bearing on the person's physical well-being: health, diseases, medications, addictions, disabilities. We include physical talents: Does the person ski? jog? bike? Is he a whiz at darts? Can he wiggle his ears? Does he play the trumpet?

How does the person spend his time? Does he work? What kind of job? What hobbies does he have? Does he watch TV? What kind of programs? Does he lie on the couch in the dark? What does he eat? Who prepares it? Does he go out much? What does he do then?

When we present body, we include not only physical appearance, but also the environment in which the person lives. Does this person live alone? In a house? How is it decorated? Is it neat or messy? What kind of food is in the refrigerator?

How does the person get around? Car? Motorcycle? On foot?

In describing body we usually mention whether the person has a family, roommates, or significant others, but we do not describe the nature of those relationships yet.

After we describe body, group members can ask questions and let us know what they are experiencing if they haven't already done so. Group members are encouraged to describe their experience, not act it out. For example, if Shelly is starting to feel as though she wants to run out of the room, she can say so, but she shouldn't really run out.

Groups find their own rhythms about speaking during the presentations. Some wait until the end of each section. Others have ongoing dialogue. We can also notice whether we have different styles when different clients are presented. I remember a student who presented a man he was working with during his internship. He said just a little bit and then seemed stuck. This is a student who usually has no trouble going on and on. We began to ask lots of questions. A couple of group members described feeling frustrated or pushed away by the student's not offering much information. It soon became clear that this was exactly what happened when the student was with this client: he asked lots of questions and got few responses. He often ended up feeling pushed away. We began to wonder if the client felt this way too.

Speech

Next, the presenter goes on to the speech section. Speech includes all of the ways that the client interacts with others. It includes actual speech as well as how the client engages in relationships. It also includes the client's emotional life since this is such a big part of our relationships. We describe all that we can of how the client talks, his tone of voice, the speed of his speech. We look at the kinds of words the client uses: elaborate? simple? slang? profanity? If the presenter can do it, we ask for an imitation of how the client might sound.

What emotions does this person feel? What emotions does he seem to not feel? Anger? Jealousy? Pride? Sadness? Elation? Appreciation? How does he express them? Or not? An important question here is how we feel when we are with this client. Do we look forward to our times together? Do we dread them? Do we feel lost? Sad? Confused? Angry? What is our relationship like? How do we spend our time together? What emotions come up? What thoughts? How do we feel right now as we present him? How are people in the group feeling as they hear about this?

What are the person's important relationships? What are they like?—remembering to be descriptive! "Jenny and her mother fight often about whether she is going to be allowed to go out." "Frank and his boss never talk about anything other than work." "Peter is very sad that he cannot fix his wife's cancer. He says he feels pretty hopeless."

As much as we can, we use what the person has told us. When we are guessing, it is good to say so. "I think Peter is feeling pretty scared, but he hasn't really said so." If we use a word like depression, what do we mean by it? Staying in bed? Crying?

I like to include relationships with animals and pets in this section. Sometimes a seeming loner has an important relationship with a dog, a cat, or some other pet. It may be the easiest place for this person to touch his heart.

Sometimes we put clothing and accessories in speech instead of in body since they are often an expression of the person, not just a way of covering the body. Either place is okay. Sometimes I am intrigued by women's handbags or men's choice of belts. Big handbags with lots of stuff in them? Little ones? Matching their shoes? Belts with small buckles? Big buckles with the names of a favorite team? These can be as personally expressive as speech.

Presentations sometimes get lost in the intricacies of the person's various relationships. The group can be helpful here. Group members can keep the presenter on the task of describing and not interpreting. It is very tempting to offer our opinions about the client's relationships. However, it is generally more useful to present them without our views. Often we find we cannot quite distinguish between our own feelings and our opinions, but this format can help us. "I feel scared when Patty goes out with her boyfriend" is quite a different statement from "Patty's boyfriend is no good for her." What is the presenter scared of? What has happened to make him feel this way? Is this his own issue or is this really about Patty?

Mind

Finally, in the mind section of the presentation we become interested in the client's state of mind, the nature of his awareness, the assumptions he makes about himself and the world, what he thinks about. An important aspect of the mind section is to identify what mindfulness and mindlessness practices the client has. What does the person know about coming into the present moment?

Is the client clear-headed? Is he confused? How often is he one or the other? Does the client notice details? Does he focus narrowly or does he have a lot of panoramic awareness? What does he assume about himself? Does he think he can do what he sets out to do or does he assume that things never work out for him? What does he assume about the world? Is his outlook optimistic or cynical? Does he assume that people are self-absorbed or does he think that people generally care about each other?

A gimmick we sometimes use in the mind section is to describe the person's mind as a kind of landscape. Is it an open meadow with a warm sun shining? Or is it a dark cavern with slithering snakes that can't be seen? Is it crowded like the attic of an old house or is it spacious, but bleak, like a swept-out storeroom?

I remember a presentation I did once, to just one other person, of a woman I was having a difficult time with. I was at my wits' end in the relationship and so asked a friend to do a body-speech-mind session with me. When I got to the mind portion, I found that an image arose in my mind of a vast, desolate desert. Feelings of deep sadness and loneliness came up with this image. I wondered if this was how the mind of the woman I was presenting might seem to her. Whether it was accurate or not, it profoundly shifted my relationship with her, and I was able to meet her the next time with a more open mind and a softer heart.

Clarifying the Exchange

The idea throughout the presentation is to allow the relationship, together with the exchange that it evokes, to arise. The feeling of the exchange might be different for different members of the group. This is good. What one member may pick up on, another might not. I do a group with students and a colleague of mine. Sometimes I exchange with the "craziness" of the client (our students often work with people suffering from severe mental disturbances), while she is able to stay with the practical details of guiding the presentation. Other times I get to be the practical one while she finds herself feeling angry or anxious.

Whatever arises lets us be more curious about the relationship between the helper and the client. Perhaps the feelings being exchanged with are those of the presenter. Perhaps they are a reflection of the client. The more clearly we can identify our experience, the more information the presenter has.

Of course, a powerful source of information for the presenter is his own experience as he presents. Often the presenter finds that he identifies with the client quite strongly. He may be able to speak for the client in a way that he couldn't before. As we have seen earlier in the book, the more we can understand of what it is like to be in someone else's place, the more we can tap into our natural compassion.

As the presentation continues, sometimes presenters can identify how they might be holding back with particular clients.

Often this occurs because they do not want to experience pain—do not want to fully enter the exchange. Recognizing this can let presenters open more or, on the other hand, realize that there may be ways that they are not willing or able to be fully present with this client now. There is no blame in this. We are trying, as always, to see what is happening and bring our mindfulness and maitri to it. We do not have to berate ourselves when we discover how we are holding back. It is good to become clear about the limitations of the help we can genuinely offer.

As the exchange becomes more clear in the members of the group, what often happens is that people may feel stuck. If we can work with the feeling of stuckness with touch and go, letting ourselves really feel what stuckness feels like, then sometimes things can open up.

Varieties of Body-Speech-Mind Groups

Practical matters like how often the group should meet and how many members it should have may vary a lot. We do weekly groups for training students. I am part of a group of colleagues who meet monthly, though we'd rather meet twice a month. Most groups meet for an hour and a half to two hours. A presentation can easily take that long. It is good to have enough time for the exchange to occur and for the group to settle in. This allows time for the occasions when we get stuck and then get unstuck too. As for numbers, most groups are four, five, or six people. This is large enough to provide variety but still small enough for people to have a chance to present on a rotating basis. As I mentioned, sometimes just one person presents to another. Some groups have leaders, others do not. Some rotate the leadership. The leader's job is to keep the task clear and to make sure no one inappropriately becomes the target of any arising aggression. If you have no one to do a group with, you can experiment with writing. Or you can try speaking into a recorder and seeing what arises when you play it back. Feel free to experiment!

Suggestions are sometimes offered to the presenter about how to proceed. Just as often, no suggestion or advice is given. The purpose of the group is to lend support and to clarify what is happening, not to figure anything out. In that way it is just like our sitting practice. My own experience over the years is that once I present people in body-speech-mind groups, my relationships with them shift. Perhaps the most valuable thing for me is that presenting someone always reminds me of the basic sanity that can be found in each of us.

23
Coming Back Home

As we have seen, in helping there is a rhythm of moving inward and outward, connecting with ourselves and reaching out to others. After we have extended out to others, it is time to come home again to ourselves. Just as we did at the beginning, we sit down quietly and look into what is happening with ourselves. Hopefully we have been steady in our sitting practice throughout the cycle and have not lost track of our sense of brilliant sanity. But if we have become caught up in the activity of helping or have become lost in exchange, this is the time to reconnect with our own health and goodness.

Sometimes people find it useful to participate in longer meditation programs. Others go on group or individual retreats as ways to reconnect and refresh themselves.

This time of settling down again with ourselves also provides an opportunity for working with the feedback we have received. Sometimes that feedback comes in the form of things that have been said to us directly. When we looked at working with feedback as a contemplative practice, we saw how we can benefit from tracking our experience when we hear or think about feedback we've been given. It is important to contemplate, to think about, what we've been told. If it is useful to us, we can remember it and experiment with doing things differently. If, on the other hand, after thinking about it we do not find it is helpful to us, we can simply let it go.

Burnout

Another source of feedback, information for us, is how we feel when we come back home. In particular, if we are feeling exhausted and burnt out, that is important information for us. Burnout refers to feeling tired, unappreciated, fed up, or overextended.

Often we feel burnt out because we have become confused about our intentions and our abilities. Ironically, we find ourselves doing more than we can really undertake skillfully because of our desire to be helpful. It is our genuine compassion that gets us in this fix. But usually, if we feel burnt out it is a sign that we have lost track of ourselves.

Becoming exhausted is sometimes the result of starting to ignore our bodies. We become somewhat mindless about whether we are hungry or tired. Instead of stopping and taking the nourishment and rest we need, we plow on and end up having less to offer than we would if we had taken a break. If this happens to us, sometimes it is a sign that our helping has itself become a mindlessness practice.

Jan worked in a residence for otherwise homeless people who also suffered from major mental disturbances. He took on a great many overnight shifts and offered his help whenever he could. At some point along the line he lost track of what he needed for himself. He became irritable and he scared one of the clients when he snapped at her impatiently. Jan's burnout took the form of feeling unappreciated and exhausted. After all, he'd done so much and now he was being criticized for mistreating a client! When we overextend ourselves, ignoring our own needs, we may end up being more of a problem than a help.

Gil found that he was starting to experience chest pains at work. A medical evaluation found nothing organically wrong. He was encouraged to relax more at work. In his job he often dealt with one person after another who brought him problems to solve. When he focused on being more present he realized that he rarely connected with people, often he didn't even say hello. Once he noticed how he was relating only to the problems, and not to the people, he slowed down and took the time to be there with others. He found that he felt less harried and the chest pains let up.

Another big source of burnout comes from unrealistic expectations. Instead of being present with the situation as it is, we start to imagine what could be happening if only we did the right thing. "If only Zoie would leave that drunken abusive husband of hers, then she would be all right." Well, Zoie has not left him. After all our efforts, she has decided to stay. Zoie is not ready to take this step for many reasons. If we are caught up with our own agenda, we will not be able to hear her or help her. We may feel burnt out. If we have built plans for someone else based on our own desires—even if they are compassionate ones—we can become fed up and tired.

When our expectations are based on ego, then we can really cause ourselves trouble. If we have fantasies of being great helpers and saviors, we will probably be disappointed. For example, I find that if I have any kind of self-aggrandizing fantasy going, I usually fall flat on my face. Once I had a client whom I had worked with for a while. Prior to our last session before she left town, I had entertained a daydream in which she would come in and thank me for being such a big help. She might even bring me a small gift. I was feeling quite self-satisfied. Instead, she showed up furious and upset. She had just had a terrible morning fraught with all the same issues we had been working on for a year. "This hasn't been any help at all!" she cried. So much for my patting myself on the back.

When we find that we are becoming burnt out, it is important to remember all the stages of the cycle of helping. Usually we have become caught up in connecting with others and with taking action and have forgotten about settling down and examining our intentions and understanding. Sometimes it is hard to break the momentum that leads us to burnout. It may seem that we are too busy or too tired to do our sitting practice. This is one reason it is important to work steadily with our mindfulness-awareness. Sitting helps us recognize the signs of burnout earlier and is also a good way to cut through some of its causes.

Letting Go

Coming home to ourselves is also the time to let go. Sometimes we have to recognize that we have gone as far as we can. We may have been working with a friend who has been feeling quite depressed and has been talking of suicide, for example. We haven't known what to do. The time we have spent being a mindful companion has been of value, but she is still talking about killing herself. This is a time when we need to call in professional help. We need to let go of any idea we have that we can do it all ourselves. If we cannot let go in this way, we may make things worse.

Letting go can also be difficult in less dangerous situations. Perhaps we have been trying to assist and support an employee of ours. Despite numerous feedback sessions and the extension of second chances, this person continues to come late, not to do his work properly, and not to learn from his mistakes. It may be extremely painful to tell this person the truth: "You're fired." Not only is it painful to tell him, but we also have to let go of our belief that we could make him change. This time there's no Hollywood ending.

Sometimes letting go is hard because we *have* been helpful. We are reluctant to give up this satisfying role. Parents may find themselves in this position. If they've done a good job, their children will be ready to take their place in the world. They will leave. As they become increasingly independent and confident, it is not always easy for us to let go. This letting go may be quite bittersweet. We wish them good fortune, yet we wonder who we are now.

Sitting practice also helps us to let go. When we find we are feeling burnt out, it is important to take the time to eat well, to get enough sleep, and to exercise. Engaging in activities that help us synchronize body and mind can be refreshing. Talking mindfully with others about how we are doing is also good. We can seek out help for ourselves.

Two Self-Supervision Techniques

Additionally, there are two techniques that can be useful to us in examining what we've been doing. One of these is process notes, and the other is a self-supervision contemplation.

Process notes are used by contemplative psychotherapists as a way of clarifying what has gone on in a particular session. We take a sheet of paper and draw a line from top to bottom dividing it into two equal halves. On the left side we write down what has happened, just as though it were a script from a play. We put both what was said and whatever actions occurred. So we put first one name and the words spoken (as well as we can remember them), and then the next name and so on. On the right side of the page we put down what we were feeling or thinking at the time the words were said.

This gives us a chance to recognize what has happened in the exchange. It also reveals to us any pattern of avoiding certain areas that the client has tried to bring up. It takes practice to get the hang of remembering what we have done and how we felt at the time. If we find that we cannot remember the right-hand side, our own process, it is an important clue that we might have been pretty mindless during the session. We might also have become so caught up in the exchange that we only "touched," and didn't "go." I often use process notes if I feel confused about what is happening with me and a client. It is a good tool for any helper who wants to sort things out. It is especially helpful because it makes us focus on what actually happened distinct from our impressions or opinions about it.

The other technique is one that evolved in a class I led one year. We had been exploring traditional methods of generating compassion (including tonglen), and we came up with the following exercise of our own. Many students have found it helpful. We begin by sitting quietly. Then we close our eyes and imagine that we are sitting across from someone with whom we are having a very hard time. We try to get a good sense of the other person, visual or not. Then we change places in our mind with the other person. Now we are the other person (let's call this person the DP for "difficult person"), looking back at ourselves. Now, as the DP, what complaints do we have about the person we are now looking at? Next, we think of what we would like from that person. What would help us? How do we feel wanting it? Now, we imagine that we receive what we want. We notice what this feels like too. Finally, we shift places again and go back to being ourselves. How do we feel now as we think of the so-called difficult person?

Many people find that they soften toward the problem person. Others discover new ways to help. Still others discover obstacles to working with the person that suggest that someone else might be a better helper in this situation. This might lead to referring them to another helper.

Continuing

As in all cycles, there is no real ending to the cycle of helping. Sitting down with ourselves is followed again by contemplating what we are trying to do. Even as we become comfortable with the fruits of our contemplation, it is time to venture out again. When we become confused, we can reflect back on all the stages of the cycle: have we settled down with ourselves? are we clear about what we are trying to do? are we really willing to communicate? is our action based on being present? are we recognizing brilliant sanity?

If we continue to practice mindfulness and awareness, we will discover again and again within ourselves the longing to be of help. If we bring to our own experience both the fearlessness to look at ourselves and the gentleness to befriend what we find, we will have tremendous wealth to share with others. Our perseverance in these simple practices can profoundly benefit others as we invite them, too, to develop mindfulness of the present moment and gentle maitri toward who they are.

Appendix A
Seeking Additional Help

THERE MAY BE MANY OCCASIONS when helpers can benefit from additional advice. There are other times when the services of helping professionals are essential. All professional helpers have other professionals to whom they turn for counsel and to whom they refer clients when they themselves do not have the expertise to help. Helping can be very difficult; we do not have to do it alone. Here are some guidelines for seeking additional assistance.

Danger

When people threaten danger to themselves or to others, we should seek assistance. If danger seems imminent, we can call emergency mental health services or the police. Calling 911 is a good choice if we do not know what else to do. Never ignore a suicide threat. Never ignore a threat to harm someone else. Licensed professionals are not held to confidentiality in such cases. In fact, they are required to alert the appropriate people. The intended victim of violence must be warned. Nonprofessional helpers would do well to follow these same guidelines.

Medical Emergencies

Generally it is better to err on the side of providing emergency care rather than holding back. Anytime someone has taken an overdose or unknown quantity of pills or other medicine, it should be treated as an emergency. When children or others swallow dangerous or unknown substances we should call poison control centers or emergency hospital services. When people collapse or become disoriented, we should seek medical advice. We can call their health care providers or we can call hospital emergency centers. We can also call 911. When we are not sure if it is an emergency or not, we should get help.

Child Abuse

In cases of physical or sexual abuse, the proper authorities should be notified. It is more important to protect the child than to worry about offending the parent or perpetrator. In most communities this means calling the area's social services department. If we are in doubt about whom to call, we can call local government offices or the police.

People Unable to Care for Themselves

When adults cannot take care of themselves, we should make sure they receive the proper professional care. This may be medical or psychological care. We may be able to provide what is needed, but a good evaluation should be done so everyone knows what is happening and what will be needed. In less dramatic circumstances, it may be appropriate to seek help if people cannot take care of their usual responsibilities, like going to work or taking care of their children. In such cases, we should probably seek professional help unless the cause is obvious and reasonable, like grieving for a recent loss or recovering from an injury.

In over Our Heads

If for any reason we feel that we have taken on more than we are able to handle, we should seek help. Many communities offer assistance on emergency hotlines, not only to those in trouble, but also to those who are trying to help. If the people we are trying to help are open to it, we should try to get them to seek professional help themselves. Many professionals will provide a free initial consultation. We can help by assisting them in deciding whom to call or helping them make calls. We can provide rides. We do not have to abandon people, but we should not carry more than we actually can.

If people tell us that they will not accept professional help under any circumstances, we need to get help for ourselves in the situation. We can then receive advice about how to proceed. If it is a situation of danger, follow the guidelines above.

When in Doubt

If we are not sure if we need help or not, we can seek assistance. It is often better to get help earlier rather than later. Many times one visit to a professional can help us, and those we hope to help, sort things out and then we can continue on our own. Just knowing that professional help is available as a backup can let us feel more confident in proceeding.

Keeping Secrets

As helpers we are often asked to keep things confidential. Sometimes we need to break this secrecy. In situations of danger or abuse, we should not agree to keep secrets. We can say so. Or, if danger requires it, we can agree to keep silence but then break it to protect the person in danger. Dealing later with issues of trust is preferable to allowing someone to be injured or killed. In general, it is not a good idea to be a holder of secrets who is expected to serve as a messenger between people who do not speak to each other. Getting caught in the middle in this way is not only difficult, it is usually not helpful in the long run since it perpetuates a pattern of not dealing with things directly. It is better to put our energy into getting people who need to talk to each other to do so.

Assorted Nonemergency Situations

We can get help for ourselves as helpers by calling various support groups. Many organizations provide information and support groups both for patients and also for the caretakers of those with different physical illnesses. There are also consumer groups providing support to the families of those with major mental illnesses. Phone numbers and addresses can be found online or by checking libraries or medical centers. Hospices have groups to support caretakers and families of the dying. Twelve-step groups provide support for addicts and their partners. Codependency groups can provide help for those who are caught in helping as a mindlessness practice.

Other Resources

It is often appropriate or comforting to call for help from religious leaders such as pastors, priests, and rabbis. Sometimes people need good legal advice from attorneys. Many communities have Legal Aid services that provide inexpensive, and even free, legal advice. Schools provide various support services including guidance counselors. Universities provide a wide range of services, often to the community as well as to their own staff and students. Many workplaces have employee assistance programs (EAPs) that provide a range of services including information and counseling. Hospitals, libraries, social service agencies, fire departments, police, physicians, psychologists, family therapists, counselors, dentists, nurses, and veterinarians are among the resources that can provide additional advice.

Appendix B Contemplative Psychotherapy Training at Naropa University

SINCE 1976, THE NAROPA UNIVERSITY, a contemplative school in Boulder, Colorado, has conducted a clinical training program leading to a master's degree in psychology: contemplative psychotherapy. Contemplative psychotherapy may be said to have two parents: the wisdom traditions of Buddhism and Shambhala and the clinical traditions of Western psychology. The three-year program combines intellectual study, meditative practice, and community interaction. Each incoming class has approximately thirty students who travel through their training together.

The training of the contemplative psychotherapist begins by providing opportunities for students to become intimately familiar with both sanity and confusion in their own experience. Through the practice of sitting meditation, the maitri program (see below), and formal study of the mind in sanity and disturbance, students become more at home with the varieties of psychological experience in themselves and also in others.

This increasing ability to be with oneself and others provides the ground for studying and practicing the clinical skills necessary for entering into genuine therapeutic relationships with clients. In the second year of the program students focus on developing these skills. In the third year, students do a nine-month internship in community agencies as well as participate in small group clinical tutorials with department faculty.

Throughout the program students participate in process groups with class members. These groups provide the opportunity for students to receive support and feedback from others, to learn about themselves as group participants, and to develop mindfulness and awareness in interpersonal interactions.

Students spend a total of ten weeks during the program living together as a learning community. Held in a scenic setting away from Boulder, the "Maitri programs" include intensive sitting and walking meditation, the introduction of tonglen practice, study, and the maitri space awareness practice. Space awareness practice is done in each of five rooms. Each room is a different color (white, blue, yellow, red, or green) and tends to intensify different emotional and psychological states—both their wisdom aspects and their confused aspects. The purpose of the maitri program is to provide an opportunity for students to come to recognize their own patterns, to become friendly toward themselves in different states of mind, and to develop genuine humor and compassion toward themselves and others. Students spend four weeks in the maitri program in each of the first two years of the program. The contemplative psychotherapy training ends with a week in the Maitri program.

I have been a core faculty member at Naropa University since 1983, and I was the director of the contemplative psychotherapy program for fifteen years. My enthusiasm for this approach is probably already apparent.

It has been my observation that being a part of the contemplative psychotherapy community, both for students and for faculty members, can be both delightful and irritating. It is wonderful when I feel supported and accepted for who I am. On the other hand, it can be awful when the same people are there again and again, and they know all about me!

Over the years I have seen our students develop confidence in themselves and in their clinical skills. Often this leads to relaxation with oneself and fearlessness in working with others. If all has gone well, upon graduation students feel ready to make a meaningful contribution to the well-being of others as counselors and psychotherapists.

For more information, contact:

Naropa University
2130 Arapahoe Avenue
Boulder, CO 80302
(303) 444-0202
www.naropa.edu

Appendix C Meditation Center Information

TO RECEIVE INFORMATION on meditation instruction (as introduced in this book) and related programs, contact one of the following:

Shambhala International
1084 Tower Road
Halifax, NS
Canada B3H 2Y5
Phone: (902) 425-4275
Website: www.shambhala.org. Information is available on the website about the numerous centers affiliated with Shambhala.

Shambhala Mountain Center
4921 Country Road 68C
Red Feather Lakes, CO 80545
Phone: (970) 881-2184
Website: www.shambhalamountain.org

Karmê Chöling
369 Patneaude Lane
Barnet, VT 05821
Website: www.karmecholing.org

For more information about the MA in contemplative psychotherapy offered by the Contemplative Counseling Psychology Department at Naropa, contact:

Naropa University
2130 Arapahoe Ave.
Boulder, CO 80302
Website: www.naropa.edu
The contemplative psychotherapy program's website is: www.naropa.edu/academics/graduate/psychology/macp/index.cfm

Index